All the Girls

All the Girls

✦

An un-manicured Memoir

Kellyann Coveny

iUniverse, Inc.
New York Lincoln Shanghai

All the Girls
An un-manicured Memoir

Copyright © 2007 by Kellyann Coveny

iUniverse books may be ordered through booksellers or by contacting:

iUniverse
2021 Pine Lake Road, Suite 100
Lincoln, NE 68512
www.iuniverse.com
1-800-Authors (1-800-288-4677)

The views expressed in this work are solely those of the author and do not necessarily reflect the views of the publisher, and the publisher hereby disclaims any responsibility for them.

Cover Design by Milk
Cover photography by Greg Delves

ISBN: 978-0-595-44284-3 (pbk)
ISBN: 978-0-595-88613-5 (ebk)

Printed in the United States of America

All the Girls are dedicated to
all my boys
Joe, Leo and Finn
You are the loves of my life.

My deepest gratitude to
my mother and father for loving me in all my incarnations,
my sisters Kristin and Amy for their unfaultering love and friendship,
my grandfather, William Sharon for introducing me to Emily Dickinson,
Charlie Tyler for being the first person to find beauty in my poetry and
Linda Stolo, the woman who gave me the faith to finally exit my darkness.
Thank you all. I could never say it enough.

Contents

Introduction

You wouldn't have liked me as a child. I didn't. I was introverted, serious and intolerant of anything resembling imperfection. French braids never sat over my cowlicks correctly. My poems never fully communicated my genius. And children my own age were unbearably young and inexperienced. I was also terrified 'it' would ever work out. I'd wrap my dog in tons of blankets and tell her over and over that it was all going to be okay. I'd sit in the back of my closet on a pile of dirty clothes waiting for someone to notice I was missing. And all my stick figure people had twenty fingers and toes so they could get 'it' all done. Still not quite sure what 'it' was. Finally I'd start all books with the last chapter so as not to experience the horrible anxiety of not knowing how things would turn out.

I stormed into early adulthood with arrogance, insecurity and the unerring belief that I was still a grossly misunderstood genius. I should warn you now this last part still lingers a bit. But overall as a now 30 something (latish 30 something) adult I can say I have finally adjusted to not growing any extra digits and I rarely wrap my dogs in blankets. The craziness about not knowing how 'it' will all work out persists.

A few other things I forgot to mention I zig-zag a lot. There's always a point but it's never a straight line getting there. And I have trouble plotting things out according to dates or events so you won't see much of those. Lastly, I lived in my head a lot as a child and so imagination plays a relatively formidable role.

The first part is about what's happening now—the day-to-day dilemmas that make me wonder what I am doing with my life. It's not really much more complicated than that. I am just your run-of-the-mill mother with dreams I am terrified of ignoring and terrified of embracing. Just your average artist with flagrant insecurities, a demanding ego and unfathomable standards. Just your typical career woman trying to balance the world on the head of a pin. Not much more complicated than that.

Part two is a little tougher to explain. This is where I listen to all the crazy voices inside my head. These are all the girls. Before you become completely freaked out. Let me explain. It is actually kind of a funny story. My then just divorced, broke boyfriend (we'll call him Joe) and I were living in my parents' guest cottage while he was trying to start his ad agency. We'd both recently lost our jobs and hadn't been able to adjust our twenty thousand dollar a month penthouse/Porsche lifestyle fast enough to fend off bankruptcy. Luckily my parents offered us their guest cottage till we could get back on our feet.

So there we were in the middle of nowhere with no money and no real idea of how we were going to make more. Throw in my parents Jack Russell terrier, Mad Maximillion running around behind Joe's desk disconnecting computer wires barking at mice in the walls and it becomes easy to see how Joe's nerves became frayed. His frayed nerves turned him just the slightest bit sour. And I was patient about it, for a week or two. But after the third week I broke down. Who the hell has moved in with me, I asked, and where the hell did my boyfriend Joe go. His answer changed my life.

Johnny he said, Johnny Wigwam. Joe will not be back for a few weeks. Don't know what to tell you. He said it without a hint of a smile. And we looked at each other for a minute. And I burst out laughing. Why the hell not? Why the hell couldn't he invent or get in touch with this shady character who made me crazy but made him feel like perhaps there was a light at the end of the tunnel. And there and then the seed was planted. There were voices inside my head, other characters, other parts of myself I had always considered too obnoxious or over-the-top or inappropriate or fancifully absurd to recognize.

The third part is about the realization of my dream. It is about the lyrics and ultimately songs and someday platinum album that came from listening to these voices. I have been writing for an ungodly amount of time. It is what saved me as a child and what feeds me now. It runs deep in my blood and I would never survive without it. Several years ago I came upon the idea of writing lyrics. And they became what I want for myself, what I want to give the world, what I dream of doing. Problem was until listening to these voices and embracing these unusual sides of myself nothing came out quite the way I wanted it to. It all sounded shallow, worked at, not terribly inspiring and just the slightest bit dishonest.

And so though very different, these three parts connect in a magically illuminating way. It is not a linear story. But then how we get to know ourselves is not linear. It is awkward, often involuntary and in the end only through really listening—not to logic or the facts of our personal myths, but to the small voices behind them, the voices with side stories and tangents and impossibly alternative points of view, the kind of voices that at first don't seem to make sense and then later make more. These are the voices that define us as unique individuals, not as members of an upstanding society or liberal political party, not as residents of an artistic seafaring suburb or creative advertising community. It is these strange and beautiful voices that set us apart, that make us interesting and special.

And what led me to write All the Girls was the idea that these voices are universal. Everyone has them. And although most of us live in their shadows, these voices have the power to set us free, to help us step outside ourselves, to see and hear the world around us. They are the whisperings of our soul. The more we listen, the more we hear and the more complex and loving we are able to be. Because only when we hear our own voices can we really begin to hear those around us. And so I offer you my voices and hope they speak to yours.

Life is messy. This memoir is an un-manicured attempt to capture it.

I am …

My name is Kellyann. I'm not much for introductions but there are a few things you should probably know up front … I'm not sleeping a lot. The eight-week-old infant, house under construction, living in a rental thing is not all that conducive to rest. At first it seemed like a romantic notion—my husband (yes, the same previously broke guy I was living with in the cottage) and I starting our new life (outside the city/newly with baby/out of catastrophic debt and back in the black) together in an old farmhouse on a beautiful property with donkeys and a pony, not worrying about whether I'd go back to work after my maternity.

But the perfect facade began crumbling when we went over to meet our land-lord, Cornelia, and her animals. She informed us that her donkeys don't like dogs. Something about having been herders of cattle, and dogs being like coy-otes … In fact, she said if our Goldens got loose her donkeys would probably kick them to death. Of course, it probably didn't help that these were Sicilian donkeys with black crosses for manes. Not exactly the bucolic picture we'd imagined. But what about the pony, we asked? Well, nothing to worry about there. The pony is blind and deaf and named Lightning. I looked over. Light-ning was munching on grass in the lower field. Lightning, huh? Cornelia ram-bled on about hey and water and the benefits of home schooling. I smiled. And how she was recently separated and worked in a homeopathic clinic and was looking forward to having such great neighbors so close by.

Great. So, how the hell was I supposed to start listening to these inner voices with a lonely chatterbox next door. Forget the idea of getting any real focused writing done. And then our contractor quit. Well, not so much quit as embez-zled funds and had to be fired. So, two weeks into it, three months was looking more like three years. These are my circumstances. My story ... is another story.

I am an Overripe Moon on a Tide-less Sea

I am periodically plagued with this deep sense of displacement, this feeling that I will never find my way home. Now, obviously having chosen to do construction and live in a rental with a fraction of our things doesn't help, but the kind of home I'm talking about is more figurative—more a kind of spiritual or emotional home. And whenever I step too far outside myself, get too wound up in the frenetic-ness of life, it comes back.

And it's strange really because it's not like I spent my childhood as a vagabond. I lived at 6 Bon Mar Road for pretty much my entire childhood. And it was hardly a traumatic place to be. There was an island in the middle of the street that I'd retreat to on white snowy nights. Sitting against a giant oak with my best friend, Eloise, we'd listen to the deadening silence of snow falling. There was an incredible calming heaviness to it. Made even Eloise, who could be a bit high-strung, sit perfectly still. Peaceful, comforting, safe. It was halfway around the world from our house.

So, we'd sit together, Eloise and I, stretching minutes like salt-water taffy, watching the snow dance beneath the spotlight of the moon. It was a slow dance. Not like the perfectly orchestrated fox trot we did at home. More like the late-night sway of old lovers, familiar with each others' rhythm, with the to and fro of it all. Eloise and I visited this island every night but few offered this perfect combination of slanted moonlight and slow-swaying snow.

It felt like home, this place, this magical swirling of serendipity. But it wasn't the night, or the island, or the mesmerizing beauty. It was the feeling inside, the impossible quieting of my nerves, of my mind, of my heart. It was the stillness, the oneness of my breath with the world, with my perfect place in it. It

6

was the feeling that I needed nothing more, that I needed to be and do nothing more, that my soul's existence was enough. It was a feeling I rarely had and longed for more than anything else. And it was a feeling I'd find out later my parents had longed for too, each in their very separate way. They danced around their differences, around their unfulfilled childhoods, around their thirty-seven-year preamble to freedom, to divorce, to individual exploration.

And now I was filled with this same searching, struggling—can't get out of the way of my own feeling. And again, it was confusing because this summer in the late afternoon haze of seemingly endless sleepless nights, I'd felt that snowy night beneath the-spotlight-of-the-moon feeling. Shadows meandering across the lawn, the sweet smell of lilacs wafting through the window, the warm weight of my baby's head resting on my chest and our bellies rising and falling in rhythm with the setting sun, with the sweet cadence of the singing birds, with all that is right. It had felt more like home than anything else.

Now that feeling was miles away. It seemed impossible to find. It could find me. When I wasn't looking, there it was. But whenever I'd seek it out, it seemed to disappear. Perhaps I looked too fast, searched too hard. Perhaps I made it nervous. My fox trot is fierce. And I never learned the Sway. So, home feels far away, always attached to circumstance, to something outside myself. I know I am there, not by what surrounds me but by what wells up inside me. The compass is there, rather here … inside. If only I could learn to be there too.

And so I closed my eyes and decided to listen, to see if I could hear a voice inside, a voice that might guide me where I needed to go. Or at least be filled with some kind of wisdom I could take with me. And I decided I would make this listening like a prayer, a reverent meditation into the abyss. So, I listened and listened and listened and listened and listened until a voice broke through the silence …

Glinda the Gardener

"You are already there. Just look in a new direction. Home is all around you. And it happens all of a sudden," said a voice so warm it began melting my insecurity.

"Take the seasons," she said. "All of a sudden … leaves grow out of twigs and worms from the dirt. And the subways' metal ceiling strips rust long rows of arbor trees.

"And then all of a sudden scraggly thorn bushes blossom over with sweet red berries and little yellow kernels sprout from giant ears. And God whistles to us in the passing train.

"Then all of a sudden there are orange faces everywhere with glowing white eyes and mouths. And the coffee lady at Hudson and Houston finds her smile.

"And all of a sudden there is a white blanket covering the earth. And buried under every white flake, a new beginning, an unlikely home to some currently sleeping miracle," she said, obviously pleased by my lowering shoulders.

"Everything was sweet," she continued, "not like sugar or processed little pieces of heaven but like giant-size miracles, like the juice of a perfectly ripened blueberry not devastated by the storm or devoured by the hungry birds … sweet like the faces in the electrical outlet smiling without mouths or the left-over dreams in the dog's crusty eyes. I used to notice these things all the time," she said.

"Now, with all my gardens, it feels like the only thing I notice is weeds. And they are everywhere. It seems all I do all day long is weed, weed, weed. My name is Glinda, Glinda the Gardener. And I clear clutter. That's what I do. It's not glamorous but without the paring back it's hard to see what's really there. It takes so long because I work in over a hundred gardens. Some are very small, some vertical and hard to reach. There's Urbania and Suburbia, Cosmica and Earthica, Domestica, Famlilica … it's silly to go on. Plus, new ones crop up every day. They all end in "A" because Utopia does, and it is my job to turn each garden into a mini-utopia. So, all the different gardens in my charge are in some way, if I can clear through all the clutter and whack those weeds into subservience, they are in some way Utopia.

"The weeds grow back so damn fast. Even when you pluck 'em from the moist ground straight from the root—even when you think you have their birth rite and procreating powers in the palm of your hand, you don't. Sometimes not even a full day goes by before an ugly green head pokes itself out of the earth and asks you to notice it over the beautifully flowering garden—and it's hard not to, lone weed like that. And harder still not to notice a pack of weeds or a field of weeds over the flowers that grow between them.

"Sometimes I get the garden cleared long enough to throw a sensational soirée where I invite all the girls and give them a tour of all the magnificent gardens, but coordinating it all just right is nearly impossible and doesn't happen often enough. In fact, the girls are always begging me to entertain more. Apparently my garden parties are the most joyous around. So, I try but they don't understand the enormous work that goes into preparing such joy.

"Some have offered to weed in their neighborhoods and I have seen them clear bits and pieces here and there. But in the big picture it's barely noticeable. Don't get me wrong, all help is welcome. It's just such an overwhelmingly enormous commitment. You have to be quite passionate.

"One day, Thandie, who you'll probably meet later, made a rather radical suggestion. She proposed the two of us throw a very intimate garden gathering where we'd notice nothing but weeds—pay homage to the clutter, focus on the beauty of that which we usually shun and embrace it, will from it fun. Just for one day. And reluctantly I agreed. We invited only those I felt would reserve judgment on what I still couldn't help feeling like was my mismanaged, unkempt garden. After all had arrived and we were standing on the flagstone path observing the overgrown weeds the strangest thing happened. The weeds levitated out of the ground and began to dance elaborately choreographed routines with mesmerizing, simple steps and we watched as they danced and danced and danced. And when they were done and we were drunk from their joy, they lay neatly on top of one another in the wheelbarrow. And our gaze remained frozen, not on the perfect garden, but its home away from home."

I understood what Glinda was saying. Yet still there was this overwhelming
feeling that I would never truly figure out how to feel at home inside myself.
But after writing this song it came to me.
Somewhere between the flowers and the weeds and the spotlight of the moon
came the realization that the fear had to do with simply stepping out of it.

Standing In the Spotlight of the Moon

I know the sand will again feel warm
It's just been so very, very long
and the wind is whipping the ends of my hair
and I can't seem to remember why
I've come all this way to clear my head,
can't remember why I got out of bed,
why I can't see through the red
to the fire burning back home.

Standing in the spotlight of the moon
unable to shake this December for June.
Standing in the spotlight of the moon
so much pressure in so small a lune …
And I'm afraid of trading cold for warm
of stepping outside this inner storm.
afraid my toes aren't up to the feat of walking the long way home.

It's not the distance that gets me down
just a summer sprint with seagulls around,
it's more the thought that I just may drown
in the spinning around of all left undone
the unwritten novel, the unstolen fun
so far from where I'd meant to be

lost on such a beautiful sea
searching for the me I'm longing to see.

So, I'm standing in the spotlight of the moon
trying to shake this December for June.
Standing in the spotlight of the moon
so much pressure in so small a lune …
And I'm afraid of trading cold for warm
of stepping outside this inner storm.
afraid my toes aren't up to the feat
of walking the long way home.

I try to run but my heart beats still
can't get up this dune of a hill
I need to feel the fire back home
but the warmth feels miles away
and I'm scared the closer I get
the more it's like a dream
and I'm afraid of stepping out
of the moon's soft beam,

So, here I stand in the spotlight of the moon
trying to shake this December for June.
Standing in the spotlight of the moon
so much pressure in so small a lune …
And I'm afraid of trading cold for warm
of stepping outside this inner storm.
afraid my toes aren't up to the feat
of walking the short way home.

I am an Oreo Overdose in Witness Protection

I will never have a normal relationship with food. What I put away last night in cookie consumption is not measurable in anything less than sleeves. Yes, sleeves, plural. And it really doesn't matter that I scraped out the stuffing of at least twenty because after the first dozen there's no such thing as mitigating circumstances. The consequences of such an act are catastrophic, no matter what.

The sheer quantity of processed sugar intake is beyond any kind of calorie count. I couldn't even wager an estimate in punitive damages. Seven hundred miles on the treadmill? Eight hundred? Who knows the punishment for such gluttony. It wasn't my first overdose and it certainly won't be my last. The difference this time was that I didn't care. It was like the crime had secured amnesty or been admitted into witness relocation and had been wiped clean from the record.

Why? That was the question. Usually escapades like this were punishable by guilt-ridden "back on the wagon" plans consisting of nothing but steamed broccoli and broiled chicken, especially given my post-pregnancy condition. Or there was the "stop being a pathetic undisciplined slob" sentence involving brutal workouts running uphill with leg weights while doing bicep curls. But this morning, I subscribed to neither. Woke up full of forgiveness.

Forgiveness was not exactly one of my strong suits, especially self-forgiveness. I was more likely to pout, stew or berate myself for such behavior. To have such a nonchalant response to so egregious an infraction was truly shocking. I mean don't get me wrong, it felt good, felt nice not to be such a terrible disappointment to myself. But it did make me just the slightest bit nervous. Was I just giving up?

Was this how people slipped from self-respecting individuals to Mall of America talk show trash? Pretty soon I'd be wolfing down bag after bag of my coveted lime-flavored tortilla chips washed down with generic soda and cheap chocolate until all my teeth rotted out and I wouldn't be able to drag my body off the couch. I'd stop brushing my hair and eventually just cut it all off when the mats started getting too thick. And my beautiful belly would slowly and then very quickly become jean-overhang. I'd quit my job and start watching back-to-back Wheel of Fortune. My bank would eventually evict me and I'd be forced to go to Key West and think up magic tricks to perform on the pier. Maybe I should just go straight there and save myself the trouble.

It was always a one-way ticket for me, this relaxed, laid-back, easygoing attitude. I could go there for hours, on rare occasion even a full day but it was so completely out of character. It always felt like if I really let go, really let me have my way with myself, I would self-destruct. I would spiral into a deep dark hole I could never pull myself out of. So even after brief, albeit dreamy, respites like this I knew I'd wake up again tomorrow with my back against the wall, no room to move.

And this little piece of self-awareness I had fought a long time to get to was responsible for the pre-emptive listening that followed. If nothing else I have tried to learn that highs like this were best celebrated with an eye to the self-judgment that usually followed.

And so I listened out, and then slowly after a while listened in for a way to give myself room when this burst of euphoria wore off.

Aphrodite the Dater

"Move to a new room and don't take it all so seriously ... there are always options ... in fact, it's all about options ... monogamy is sooo monogamous ... that's why I serial date," said a seductively sweet voice to whom sentences seemed more like hills than structured thoughts.

Her voice was hypnotic but I wasn't so sure where she was going with the whole monogamous-less thing.

"It began with drapery treatments," she continued, "the idea that you could keep an arsenal of drapes in the mix and rotate them in and out depending on your mood and the season ... and I thought what if you could do this with men ... what if you could shift out boyfriends as the mood struck ... what if boy-friends could be drapes? It was a very big thought, worthy of some kind of the-sis or editorial feature or fortune cookie ... so, I obsessed about it until reality hit. There would never be enough men. So, why not expand the dating pool to include all things worthy of joy and pain—high heels, ice cream, exercise pro-grams, therapists ... create a harem of harems," she said, running out of breath.

"Oh yes, my name is Aphrodite the Dater," she added absent-mindedly.

"Anyway, dating is such an epic proposition, the condensed version like a TV mini-series of Greek mythology ... and you usually just keep playing the same roles over and over again depending on your type—the dumper, the dumpee, the jealous rager, the lusty adulteress ... there is no moral or lesson or ultimate philosophical point ... in fact, if you try and make one you end up dating the very idea of dating itself.

"Currently I am dating names for my pet peacock. Nothing definitive yet ... tried Fernando and Giancarlo and Sir Camelot but not sure of his heritage ... anyway, nothing is sticking quite yet but that's the beauty ... if it doesn't feel right, you keep going till it does ... it's like baking cookies or pitching base-balls ... and I've set my sights very high. Must be aristocratic but not preten-tious, strong but not stiff, romantic but not soft ... so many criteria. It's an art really. I had a perfect girl name picked out … three actually … but boys are trickier. No great shock there. Anyway, have one or two and still dating others … waiting for the perfect fit.

"I dated Mint Chocolate Chip ice cream for like fifteen years. Thought for sure it was my true love but then quite suddenly I began to find bright green a bit garish and the chips not quite flavorful enough and I became disillusioned with the sheer simplicity of it and so I moved on to Coffee Oreo Swirl. Sophisticated but fun, childlike with an adult flare. It seemed to me what down-to-earth fashionistas might eat but boredom set in quickly and I started dating all kinds of flavors desperate to find the one truly meant for me at this most evolved point of my life. I couldn't reconcile the ones that made me happy from the ones that felt sophisticated. There was Vanilla Brownie Fudge in one camp and Dark Chocolate Pistachio in the other … there were the ones I could eat by the pint and ones where one scoop was enough and I could not choose between the two. I thought I would be destined forever to indecision, to a life of duplicity. I watched strangers on the street enthralled with their Dulce de Leche and friends gaga over their Chunky Monkey and I longed for the perfect blend of everything in my flavor and suddenly there it was, in the grocer's case at the Food Emporium—Mint Oreo ice cream. So simple. So obvious. And yet there it was. Not where I had hoped to find it, not the kind of name I had dreamed of but the flavor I had always longed for," she said wistfully.

To not take it all so seriously—this is a huge challenge for a girl like me.
What if self-love could exist
without planning for the imminent onslaught of self-judgment?
What if there were other options?
What if there was room between the two extremes
for possibilities I hadn't even considered.

It Happens

It happens …
it happens …
it happens, it happens, it happens …

It was an accident, he fell asleep
we hadn't planned it out
but his body, heart and mind
were now within my care,
his everlasting dreams
were somehow ours to share.
So, I threw the list to do away
simply decided to stay.

It happens
when moments free themselves of time
it happens
when there's no agenda to define.
It happens, it happens, it happens
when you expect nothing from now.
It happens, it happens, it happens
you can't imagine how.

All the Girls

My baby's chest, his quiet breaths
so peaceful in my arms
the branches out the window
so naked in their charm.
My heartbeat coming slower
now warmer in my chest
the squirrel's flying higher
at its acrobatic best.

It happens
when moments free themselves of time
it happens
when there's no agenda to define.
It happens, it happens, it happens
when you expect nothing from now.
It happens, it happens, it happens
you can't imagine how.

Oh, the rise and fall of kings and things
so tempting in their plight
the rise and fall of everything
so full of monumental might
and yet it doesn't happen here
the things we hold forever dear.

It happens
when moments free themselves of time
it happens
when there's no agenda to define.
It happens, it happens, it happens
when you expect nothing from now.

I am an Oreo Overdose in Witness Protection

It happens, it happens, it happens
you can't imagine how.

I am a Breath That Can't be Caught …

I will never be here, now. The problem with being here is it always seems to take me to there. For example sitting here now on this brown leather chair, gray-speckled throw pillow on my lap typing on this two-year-old laptop takes me back to Mig and Tig on Illinois Street in Chicago where I purchased the pillow right after my divorce. I was putting my life back on track to move forward. And there it was—a beautiful gray chenille couch with matching pillows. And there I was with money to finally invest in my future, my self. It was quite a thing, the idea of spending money on myself. I had always put whatever I made immediately in the bank, not for a rainy day but for when I met with my inevitable financial ruin. So, today was a breakthrough day. I would throw financial ruin to the wind and spend.

It was serendipity really, this completely unplanned, unexpected empowerment that had come with my decision to leave my sweet, safe, seven-year marriage for the passion and creative integrity I ached for, for what was really the great unknown. Prior to this newfound courage, I had never been generous with myself. I allowed others to be. In fact, I strongly encouraged it, being so needy of the giving spirit I refused to give myself. It always amazed me, other peoples' ability to give without feeling, like something was being taken. It made me distrustful but neediness is a desperate thing. And fear of betrayal wasn't going to get in my way.

Anyway, I was so cheap with myself I didn't even feel worthy of cab fares. So I'd drive my scooter in rainstorms, December, the dead of night through housing projects—whatever it took to get where I needed to go without paying for it. And there was another theme: wanting something for nothing. Not that I wasn't willing to work hard, cause I was. Well, pretty hard. It was more that I didn't really believe anything would work out (see financial ruin theory) so it wasn't worth investing in unless there was some kind of shortcut.

Take my first job in advertising. I was convinced if I was charming and witty enough I could shimmy my way under the wire from the account side into the creative department with no problem. Sure, everyone else had to invest time, money, sweat and tears into their first portfolio. Not me. I'd skate my way there. In the end, of course, I had to take the long road and make the investment just like everyone else. But even then I made a deal with the portfolio school owner: I'd work part-time and take classes for free.

It wasn't that driving in December, windblown tears freezing on my temples or going straight from Starbucks to my second shift at the portfolio school was easier. It was simply that my time and discomfort was a safer price to pay. Money was somehow sacred and must be guarded and protected at all costs. It was as if I'd grown up in the depression or lost everything in the Gold Rush or had to eat from garbage cans growing up.

But, if I considered myself worthy enough to pursue a new life, if searching for passion and creative integrity was not a ridiculous pipe dream then maybe I was worth a fifteen hundred dollar gray chenille couch with matching throw pillows. And eight years later, back in "the here" the throw pillow had migrated from my couch to the brown leather chair my new husband had brought to our marriage.

And I imagined eight years from now, the laptop that sat on the throw pillow that sat on the leather chair would take me beyond seeing myself as a worthy financial investment into the part where I see myself as a worthy creative spirit capable of reaching great human truths. And from this same place I could see my future, see how my western silver turquoise belt buckle gleamed in the light as I shifted in my chair on Oprah's set, about to answer her question about how this all came to be. I'd smile and humbly reply with some brilliant self-deprecating piece of humor. She'd laugh and say, "Ain't that the truth sister," looking to her audience for the confirmation she knew we both had.

So, once again it came down to the question: how do you stay right here, right now when everything is so connected to everything else? How do you stay focused in this exact moment when it's your history that got you here and this moment you're hoping will take you into tomorrow? And what if Einstein was right? What if there was no such thing as time or space? What if there was no real *diem* to *carpe*? What if ...

But maybe I was just using Einstein to justify something I couldn't really do. Maybe at the end of the day, relativity was all relative, really just a quantum cut-out doll designed to avoid the fact that my mind was always racing, that I was terrified of being still, that my right foot had fallen completely asleep here on this brown leather chair at 4:43P.M. on Tuesday.

I decided to listen, not out of fear or need but more out of curiosity. And I listened and listened and soon enough heard ...

Tia the Traveler

"Sometimes the here and now is really over there. And sometimes it's farther than you ever dreamed. The key to being in the present is to play with it. See where it takes you. Take yourself on field trips," said a sing-songy sprite dressed in pink light, "like mini-vacations in a marathon moment, but not to places you've already been or surmise you later may be."

Sounded provocative and promising, depending on the field trip.

"They clear out the cobwebs without getting caught, transform confusion into clarity without a single logic link. But don't try to follow. Run with it," she said.

And she was off leaving only the trail of her voice, "I am running down our long gravel driveway. My aunt just delivered her first baby. My mum is dying. It is two thousand years ago and I am a five-year-old boy. I enter her bedroom where she has resided most of my life. I know she's leaving soon. But I am not afraid. I tell her the news. She has been waiting. The corners of her mouth twitch and I know she is trying to smile. I smile back. She closes her eyes. And I know. I climb into bed and we sleep awhile."

She paused briefly blinking to another spot and continued, "Went diving yesterday, sans oxygen tank, in deep sea grass. Like lily fields on the way to Oz, they lulled me into a slumberous sea-dream. I reached out my arm and dragged it along spiky pink coral until the cuts woke me. I swam up through a dark tunnel toward a black sun and into the base of a tree trunk. I climbed out through an owl hole and sat on the beach until a sand spider instructed me to re-enter the trunk and continue up. I did and halfway up, it split in two. I froze. Afraid of which way to go, which way not to go, afraid of not recognizing right from wrong or left, afraid of generational disappointment, I waited for a sign. None came. So, I went right (right-handed, live east, where Jesus sat) and the trunk splintered into a thousand twiggy arms. They all looked the same, and different. None were wide enough. All began and ended the same, with more choices. So, I scaled back down and went left. I started crawling and ended up running and then flying faster and faster and faster until I was in a racecar exiting the trunk tunnel and flying down a highway. I had no direction, just speed. The horizon line kept looming farther out. There were no roadside lemonade stands, no homes, no barns, no gasoline stations, just miles and miles of road. And I looked up to see God. The sky was a sea of blue with two small armchairs inside two white clouds. My mother sat to the right, my father to the left. And between them, straight ahead, lay a solid yellow line.

"I hop the pink light. It's fastest," she continued a bit more conversationally. "Leers are limited by landing strips, yachts by slips, and cars by laboriously long road trips. The pink light takes me to the heart of things in seconds. From there I let go. Imagination and divine inspiration pilot my journeys. I give them my destination, free of location. The places we go are unreachable by maps or itineraries or master plans. The destination is always far-away interior landscapes. My imagination guides me through the tundra of metaphor showing me where to turn in the blinding frenzy of reason. In the end the trips are like a field-full of fireflies illuminating the darkness.

"Like earlier this morning, I traveled to a tree at the top of a grassy knoll, a beautiful old cherry tree with arms enough for a hundred swinging children. As I approached it, I froze and began sobbing uncontrollably. I fell to my knees. Hanging from the tree were hundreds of black bodies. Young and old and dead. They hung as if posed for some future history lesson, their heads all cocked to one side or another, questioning. Their bodies hung limp and stiff. Color had drained from their faces. They were my colorless friends. I had tried to save them, one lone white woman on a crippled crusade in dark times. Their freshly sprung spirits clung to me for safety. I carried them, a hundred black ghosts, afraid of the light, through a century of incarnations. I hadn't realized they needed to be free. I let go.

"Inside the pink light is my spirit guide. My launch pads are all located on the portholes of her experience and she sees everything slant—always has. So nothing is ever quite as it appears. Every image is like a seven layer cake—lucky, delicious and too rich to ever finish."

And with that she was off again before I'd had a chance to catch my breath.

"Last week I rowed through winding rivulets, careened down twisting tributaries and docked at the entrance to the medulla. I entered and inside was this enormous piece of sushi. The right side was filled with salmon, the left with tuna. I split them apart and two fish swam away.

"Seconds later, I stopped off in the middle of a tranquil lake beside a tiny rowboat where a beautiful woman was supposed to be sitting with her lover. Instead, two black periscopes poked through the bottom of the small wooden vessel. They stretched their long metal necks turning slowly in circles observing the velvety stillness. And I realized she was with him below in a giant yellow submarine," she said double-checking that I was still with her.

"The jet lag is odd. Some trips wipe me out for days. Others warp the lag, leaving me far ahead of where I was. The trips are not subject to gravity or relativity or laws of any kind. They are more like quantum leaps into parallel universes where the present is a fog framed out by fantasy and past lives. It is the purest kind of freedom.

"There are tiny tears in the universe, tiny pink rabbit holes. I enter. The trips are short, the journeys long," she said and was off again.

The idea of here and now sometimes being over there was thought-provoking.
Add in the ability to play with the present versus just acknowledging and
accepting it, and a whole new world of travel opened up—
dreamy new landscapes that allowed me to leave my present, present behind.

Track One-Eleven

Meet me at Grand Central, track one-eleven, lower level
and we'll catch the 5:49
to a country full of sunshine.

And I'll follow your gaze wherever it goes
as the train trips bumps, touching our toes.
I'll follow the cadence of your melodious voice
as it floats above this grumbling noise.
I'll curl inside your collarbone
as we search for somewhere closer to home.

Yeah, meet me at Grand Central, track one-eleven, lower level
and we'll catch the 5:49
to a country full of sunshine.

And I'll dream of your hand on my lower back
as we rumble down this rickety track
dream of your breath on the back of my neck
as our train devours its tired old track
fantasize about your smell and mine intertwined
in that moment in time where our heartbeats rhyme

We'll head out of the city
and swim through all the pretty
pictures passing by ... pictures passing by

Yeah, meet me at Grand Central, track one-eleven, lower level
and we'll catch the 5:49
to a country full of sunshine.

I am Melba Toast in Search of Smoked Trout ...

Here is the big, self-defeating fear that grips me in the gut, usually after meeting or hearing about or reading of some fantastically fascinating person ... I will never be interesting enough to raise eyebrows. I mean what makes me so special? It's not like I'm royalty living in a big castle or a starving artist living in some glorified hovel or a Cuban refugee struggling with cultural assimilation. Who is going to care about the perspective of a college-educated homeowner with highlighted hair, a closet full of killer shoes and five-hundred-thread-count sheets? Who cares? What is unique about what I have to say? Where is the drama? The struggle? The "oh my God, you can't be serious"?

There have been no hits on any of my uncles. My mob connections are tangential at best. I've had no near-death experiences, never survived an avalanche or run across a UFO. I am not a member of any cults or shticky bridge clubs. I have taken no cross-country or LSD trips, never experimented with slot machines or lesbians. What is my point, my hook, my in? What do I have to offer that is fresh, interesting?

Nothing is my worst fear. Actually, worse than nothing would be a half-baked something that leaves you feeling nauseous and hungry at the same time. But even worse than that would be the truth. What makes me truly different, what makes any of us truly different I guess is our perspective on things. Problem was my perspective sometimes requires a troupe of translaters.

It all began in the first grade when Mrs. Nardone put on my report card that I had trouble sequencing. Seemed harmless enough. And then there were the sweet blank stares of my parents reading my poetry in sixth grade. Unnerving but whatever. And then there was the morning brunch at Sunny Side Up Diner with Joe (this is pre-wedding, pre-cottage, actually pre-financial win-fall and then ruin). He leaned in over his sausage links, told me he loved me but had no idea what I was talking about and in fact rarely did.

That's when I knew for sure. I was not "linear." Not in any way. My stories usually start at the end and then backtrack abruptly before zigzagging through tangents to get to the beginning. Part of this disjointed jumpiness was fear that I would lose my listeners interest but mostly it was just me. See, my view of things has never been terribly straightforward, never easily understandable. The ending was never really the point to me, nor the facts. It was always about some obscure observation that happened as a result of the whole experience or a powerful emotion that ran through the middle of it. Linear progression made me manically impatient. I always wanted to know the point. And the point was never the story. The point was where the story skewed left or jogged in circles or ran out on itself barefoot in the rain.

Why? That was all I really cared about. If storytelling were left to me it would be about that. No beginning. No end. Just insight wrapped sometimes in swaddling blankets of protective awe, others stripped down to their naked truth. Would depend on the strength of the insight and willingness of the audience to consider the value of something so seemingly obtuse.

Problem is most people don't like obtuse. Most people like stories, nice linear stories that start one place and go to another. And those are not the stories I have to tell. So, I'm afraid I will be exhausting more than interesting. And if I raise eyebrows, it might not be for the right reasons.

And so again I listen not at all sure this is a very kosher thing to be asking for guidance on and even less sure there will be any voice willing to respond. But as I have done before, I listen and listen and listen and listen and listen and …

Carrie Carrie Quite Contrary

"So what? I am upside-down girl," said a blustery voice attached to a very sophisticated looking Pippi Longstocking with bobby socks and a pink-and-orange plaid beret. "Course, people have called it contrary, made up entire limericks to try and make me feel embarrassed and ashamed of it but fact is, if I wasn't upside-down I'd be dead. So whatever to them."

I wasn't quite sure where she was going and longed for this to be more—linear. But the beret was becoming.

"It started a while ago. You see, Carrie rhymes with like a million trillion things but only thing kids in my neighborhood could come up with stinks. And that's being polite. If I'd been pretty or a rock-throwing little menace like I wish I'd been, they'd have left me alone. But, no, course it doesn't go like that. Anyway, their favorite stupid little limerick that they'd shout from across the street or on the hallway outside homeroom was … 'Carrie, Carrie quite contrary, how does your garden grow?' I'd scrunch up my face and walk away. But, finally, after enough jabbing I decided not to walk away. And next time they said, 'Oh Carrie, Carrie quite contrary, how does your garden grow?'

I said, "It's not a garden. The flowers have no roots. They were murdered in their sleep. So now it's just a graveyard filled with empty promises."

Carrie was a dark little girl but I rather appreciated that and was excited about where she might take me.

"I knew it was strange," she continued, "but I didn't care. Something had to change and it was quite honestly the first thing that came to mind. They stopped all wide-eyed in shock. Seemed like hours for about a minute and then it seemed more like seconds. And then they finished me off with even more of their stupid gleeful jabbing, convinced now more than ever of its truth.

"Eventually it made me want to be like all the other kids but luckily as I was plotting out how I might become Carrie, Carrie the beautifully sensible and predictable fairy, Tia stepped in and offered to take me on one of her magic destiny ball trips. We'd followed my magic ball once before so I knew what to do. I closed my eyes, tossed it up, jumped and we flew, Tia right behind us. We flew high above the earth with great purpose and direction till slowly we started descending through sky and clouds, sky and clouds, like sliding down an enormous pastel candy cane. And we slid right into the same place we had before. It was my safe place, my happy place. At first I was disappointed cause I'd been here so many times before and I wanted to go somewhere new. But she said we were, not to worry, So I didn't, for now.

"There were the same clouds full of grass and wildflowers, a small sea with a giant tortoise whose shell was my special resting spot. It was peaceful and beautiful and calming. I loved being there but wanted to know why we were returning now. So, I asked my magic destiny ball and as Tia had promised everything became different.

"The destiny ball gave me gills and took me under the shimmering surface of my sea—down, down, down to the bottom and there were thousands, maybe millions of colonies of tiny fluffy pink marshmallow-like munchkins singing and working. As I looked closer I realized they were actually not working at all. They were busy making pancakes. So, I asked what they did for work. And confused, they replied that they made pancakes of course. And I thought how silly. No one would really consider that work. It's not like you can make a living that way or work for a boss. And why would you need an assembly line to do something so simple. And I looked around for the real workers. And there were teams attaching sparklers to the edge of all the stars in their sky. And I looked around more and all these tiny creatures were somehow, some way passionately involved in the production of joy, of pleasure, of beauty. And I thought how contrary to the way the real world works. How contrary and upside-down.

"And as if reading my mind, Tia asked me what would happen to this world of mine were these creatures not to exist. And I watched the tortoise turn into an octopus and grab me with its long legs and pull me underwater where I could now no longer breathe. And I thought, without upside down, I'd be underground." And with that she skipped off quite content with her little story.

So perhaps upside-down was my version of interesting.
It seemed more strange than interesting but maybe that was okay.
Maybe upside-down was bigger than interesting.
What I didn't know until I finished this song was how desperately I needed
something bigger than an interesting hook.

Upside-down Dream

There's this story I've been trying to tell
'bout a paralyzed vigilante.
It's a personal mythology
with only one flaw
it follows a dream
that goes nowhere at all.

See I wanted to be the goddess
of upside down
wanted to be the nymph
of never-say-never-land
so many things I wanted to be
so much armor I've put on to be free, to be me.

So I keep letting go to try and hold on
softening up to try and be strong
but it all seems wrong
gotta grab my dreams—and move along.

But I keep ending up
in the middle of a field
in the middle of my head,
there I am again
searching for windmills

to blow through the pain
searching for something
to ease the strain—of this boomerang.

So, I keep letting go to try and hold on
softening up to try and be strong
but it all seems wrong, it all seems wrong
gotta grab my dreams—and move along,
take my dreams somewhere they belong,
take my dreams somewhere they belong.

I am a Winning Lotto Ticket
Buried Under the Couch …

Why I am here? What is my purpose? These heady self-reflective questions used to be reserved for late-night insomnia. Not a lot of time to address the finer points of existence with a full-time life. But things are different lately. I seem to have entered a three-month maternity fog and these questions plague me on a regular basis. The smarter part of me mocks the insanity of such deeply grandiose questions. But here I am and there they are rearing their lofty little selves again and again.

And this time, unlike college, it isn't about souped-up philosophical meanderings. The question of why I am here comes down very practically to what I should be doing with my life, which is not exactly what I am doing now. And it is a hard thing to undertake, changing your life, if you haven't recently been fired or had a near-death experience. Fighting the gravity of the status quo is a monumental undertaking and usually, at least for me, becomes paralyzing in the far-reaching ripple effect that follows. There's the dream and the reality. And the reality of the dream is that it gets put on the back burner out of responsibility. To what? A million things, I guess—making money to raise a family, not abandoning a long-time career—things like that. Or maybe it's really out of responsibility to perpetuating the illusion that the dream is impossible.

But every now and then I feel irresponsible for not taking my dreams more seriously. If I'm to make this album a reality shouldn't I quit my job and dive into it 500 percent? Or if I am going to become a screenwriter shouldn't I quit my job and just write my brains out? Or if I am going to be a professional mom, shouldn't I quit my job and start getting really involved in the community and playgroups and … never mind. Need to do the mom thing my own way. Point is, although my job is the best I've ever had, it is not my dream to write advertising. Unfortunately, with directors and editors and music houses it is just close enough to be confusing. If I worked in a bank, I'd have to quit. Course, I'd probably be fired first. And I keep the dream on life support by dedicating a few hours a week to a song here, a scene there. But is it enough? And is it why I am here?

And why does why I am here bother me so much? I think maybe because I had this feeling through my whole childhood, this aching feeling that I would invent a new language. Not like French or Spanish but more like a universally integrated, interactive language of art and love. It would not be art or writing or music but all of them. It would somehow be like a collage or montage of expression. And not like weird performance art. It would be world renown and would seem in the art world practically as vital as our opposable thumb or inner voice. That's sort of what it was going to be, an alternate way of communicating our inner voice.

The idea seems a bit daunting now and quite possibly more the desperate longing of an unheard child than a psychic premonition. But what has remained with me is this strong feeling that there is something I have to give the world that is very important both for me and the world. Could be my immediate world. Could be the world of artists. Could be the country. All I know it is my job to figure out what exactly it is I have to offer and stay committed to it. No matter how much time I give it or how much failure I encounter.

And failure is so confusing. Is it a sign that you are on the wrong path or a test to see how committed you are to your dream? For good or bad, I haven't had the option of seeing it the first way because writing, whatever kind of writing it is, is in my blood and there's not a damn thing I can do about it. It's like an invisible lung or heart. But although I could never not write, trying to get the writing sold is a whole different can of worms. The rejection part, which I've had plenty of experience with, leaves me putting songs and manuscripts in drawers rather than in envelopes on their way to opportunity. So I am left fighting the idea that why I think I am here is all really just some esoteric pipe dream.

And when I get tired of thinking writing is the answer to why I'm here, I move on to the equally challenging issue of karmic balancing. I have collected thoughts and beliefs and credos and philosophies like a bizarre collection of worldly trinkets and together they form my personal religion. Karma is one of these prized trinkets and so it is incumbent upon me to figure out what I have to learn and not screw it up so I have to do it all over again. Repetition is unbearable for me, probably a function of being bored so easily. So I have figured out pretty well what it is I need to work on and although I certainly haven't mastered any of it yet, I am on my way. Few of the biggies—not to push so hard, not to need everything to be so perfect, to be able to see some things as okay just the way they are. This last one is a big struggle.

One breast is bigger than the other. One eye is smaller than the other. And I would like to see these details as beautiful, artistic, like an exquisitely lopsided Picasso or Matisse. Like the way I see other people. But I don't. I see them as unfixable flaws that I must learn to embrace. So, perhaps I am here is to let go of all the judgment, to feel the joy of whimsical observation, curious delight, to rejoice over every little detail—to let the hell go a little. And so there is some consolation in that. Nothing I like better than a plan of action but the Part 1 in the why-I-am-here series continues to elude me.

And so the way I have done before I step back, step slowly away from controlling the question and listen for a voice to take me somewhere new, somewhere beyond my silly limitations, somewhere I can ...

Frida Rita Writer Girl

"Begin, begin, begin. It's all about beginning. Beginning. Reinvention. Just a slight shift in perspective opens up entirely new worlds. And once you get past the mudslide, it's fun," said this rather smoky voice.

I wasn't exactly sure I was up for the whole new worlds thing. Felt like I had enough of them already but lord knows I could use a little fun. So on we go.

"I am Frida Rita Writer Girl. Do not confuse me for my twin sister Tia. My world is very different. It's like a 24/7 search party … how to reach the world behind the world, the matter within the matter, the baby under the belly of reality. I am always searching for secrets, for ways out and ways in to under-standing, for meaning deeper than the membrane of because.

"I've lived in a land of underground passageways for a very long time. It was hard to get around because of the torrential rains and resulting mudslides. There were days it was impossible to get a grip of any kind. Walking was not an option. Crawling was not even an option. Some days sliding downhill was all I could do. And I'd struggle and try with everything I had not to fall all the way back down to the bottom. I'd grab hold of rocks and crags and anything that looked solid. I'd hold on for my life but there's no holding on to seven-layered mud. More like cake than skin. And I'd continue down. There was a plateau a little more than halfway down and when the slide was slower I could eek to the side and remain frightfully still until the rains stopped and when it was safe I could venture my way back up. I knew if I reached the top, no mat-ter how long it took, if I could make it above the underground there would be light and I longed for that kind of clarity.

"I live in a mythological maze that twists and turns snaking its tale of darkness through glistening tunnels of terror until mystically hitting a place so bright that there is nothing but white, a pure unbroken sea of white. All the colors come together in a wickedly bright union and once in a great while after the rains the individual colors break apart and arch their beautiful backs across the sky.

"I live in a custom-built theme park below the Big One. The water made the fabulous mudslides that wind and turn and let out in a giant mud bath. There's nothing better than sliding in mud. Gooey and goopy and darkly delicious. My only disappointment is that it does not taste better. So I slide all day and sleep on the buoyant sea of darkness. It keeps me afloat till we slide again. And unfortunately, occasionally it sometimes suns which puts a damper, rather dryer on my fun. But it's not so bad because I am covered head to foot in drying mud and there's a certain satisfaction in breaking it apart, peeling it off, flaking it away, knowing full well by the time I'm done the rains will be back and my sliding sloppier and sloppier than ever.

"I live in the buried world of Mesopotamia. The rains have washed away all their artifacts but I wander their deserted muddy streets and paths riding the waves of mud that frequently wash through them. I am trying to get a sense of their Master's Design, of the Architect's Plan—of what made this great city work when it did. I can feel in the energy of the mud they're pounding chariots and racing feet. I can feel the narrower passageways—the pitter-patter of barefoot children and when I close my eyes I can hear the booming authoritative voice of men and sense the undercurrent of feminine wiles.

"I live in rabbit holes and gofer tunnels. I followed a rabbit one day before even hearing of Alice and we went down but not so far. And he stayed but I saw a gofer go by and I followed him hoping someone would take me to the source, to the one grounded enough to get the inner workings of dirt and why it turns to mud and why we slide and how to get back up better when we slide so far down.

"I live in the upside down flight pattern of migratory birds. It is the brown reflection of their blue, their shadow perhaps. It is hard to fly through earth but I wonder if the free-fall mudslide is not too dissimilar. I hold my arms out and the mud carries me down. I don't know where they originate or where they ultimately land to nest. The distances are too far but I am getting the hang of a shorter migration. It is like commuting through mud in search of fertile ground.

"I live in a modern abstract work of art and I keep searching for hints of a representational reality or impressionistic fantasy or something more immediate and local to wrap my head around. It is strange to wander the lines and textures of someone else's imagination without the map of their experience or the pulse of their heart to inform it. So, I deduct and deduce, imagine and intuit, come to my own multiple paradoxical contradictions of what it means to live inside art."

After I got over the overwhelming multiplicity of beginnings
I think I got it—
keep writing, keep creating, keep the love alive
because things aren't necessarily as they seem
and there is outrageous possibility in absolutely everything
including the places there doesn't seem to be.

Open Your Eyes

First thing there is no second
not if you're in the game
there's something different in every detail
something different goes without fail
the way dew sits on a spider web
the way your lover tilts her head
the way frogs sound on a summer night
the way a streetlamp slants its light.

Open your eyes, open your eyes
the world has another surprise
it's not where you've been it's not what you think
defies all jaded instinct.
Yeah open your eyes, open your eyes
see what makes you feel alive.

Can't repeat a one-eyed wink
and have it be the same
there's something different in every detail
something differerent goes without fail
the way your child looks into your eyes
the way a peony gracefully dies

the way fresh tomatoes taste like sun
the way seagulls start to run.

Open your eyes, open your eyes
the world has another surprise
it's not where you've been it's not what you think
defies all jaded instinct.
Yeah open your eyes, open your eyes
see what makes you feel alive.

If you open your eyes before you see
there's a window of opportunity
to leave memory on the ledge
clear your cluttered head
see it for the first time … again.

Open your eyes, open your eyes
the world has another surprise
it's not where you've been it's not what you think
defies all jaded instinct.
Yeah open your eyes, open your eyes
see what makes you feel alive.

I am a Tired Bird in a World Full of Branches ...

This is related to the why-am-I-here dilemma but don't be confused. It is vastly different and symptomatic of an entirely additional problem. I will never be able to commit to anything. So, why is it in a world full of opportunity that I can't manage to land somewhere? Make some kind of decision and commit? The options are endless. There's the win-lose scenario where I continue pulling down my six-figure salary and just begin chipping away pieces of my soul. There's the lose-win where I cash it in and sit in my soon-to-be foreclosed house writing my heart out. There's the lose-lose, my personal favorite, where I stay home and develop a terminal case of writer's block along with a drug problem which I can't keep up because of my dwindling finances and can't kick because Betty Ford won't take my Costco Card.

And then there is, of course, the win-win where I go back to work and write my songs while commuting. I always wonder what kind of idiot wouldn't take this option. So, I keep re-selecting it and becoming just a bit more depressed and overwhelmed and helpless in my have-it-all situation. The confusion makes me begin circling again flying higher and higher to get some kind of new perspective till I am left gasping for air falling quickly back into my win-win scenario.

And of course now there's the added pressure of whether to be a good mother or a good worker-bee, to breastfeed on the couch or express pump from some janitor's closet. I know it sounds kind of like I've made a decision but I haven't. Flip-flop every other day with some new angle I hadn't considered before. I also tend to recycle angles since there are always new angles on the angles. It's like an ever-shifting prism of possibility. So why do I end up seeing nothing but planes of fear?

Then, there's the whole fear of failure part (I know we sort of covered this but it crops up a lot so bear with me) where the minute I decide to pursue the dream of creating my album, of writing inspiring lyrics, of making beautiful music, I remember there are no producers beating down my door waiting to see what I will do next. And the odds that I would manage to get a foot in any door are remote. And even if I did, the likelihood that it would amount to anything more than a small coffee over a lot of lip service is practically nonexistent. So, there's that.

On the other hand, when I decide that I will go back to work, make great money with great people at a creative job where I work great hours and shoot great spots with great directors while staying at great hotels, it occurs to me that the pit in my stomach is not from a peach.

There's also the fear of what I'll miss. And what do I give up—my song-writing dream ... adult interaction ... my baby's cooing ... mental stimulation ... finding my own voice ... ice grapes by the Shutters pool. The list goes on and on with me adding new variations usually in the middle of the night as I contemplate what I should do with my life while adjusting my breast for better "latching" potential.

Then there's the fear of not knowing what I don't know. What if writing from home is really about changing diapers and convincing the pest control people to come sooner than next week as the ants in my kitchen are putting up condos all over the house. And what if going back to work is really about fixing legal copy and testing spots until they struggle for months on life support only to quietly die one night in their sleep. Is the decision really between pest control and testing hell? And why do I never consider the unknown success scenario? Like why isn't it about me choosing between receiving my gold Cannes Lion or producing my multi-platinum album?

My issues with commitment run much deeper than just my job. My most recent dilemma is whether to go for the thirty-eight-inch Viking for six grand or the forty-one-inch Jenn Air Pro series for five? Not brain surgery really, right? Well, except for me. So, I get that three inches doesn't really make a difference. Not in a fridge. But then there's the question of aesthetics—too close to call. Image: fairly obvious. Price: completely obvious (except for the whole quality for the money aspect). Resale: arguable either way. Our refrigerating needs (notice this comes last): who cares? Considering we now stock mostly mustard, vodka and a few precious bottles of expressed breast milk, a twenty-incher would be just fine. When you line it all up there is no easy conclusion. So, I flip a coin but the other option always seems better once one is made for me. So, in the end I give up and turn it over to the only person in the house capable of making a decision without becoming comatose.

Thing is, there are decisions I must make for myself, important decisions that really impact my life, life decisions that no one can make for me, And I truly feel overwhelmed by the warring fears inside me. And the humor I use to get through it is becoming a bit more manic than offhand.

So again I close my eyes and look for a voice to speak to me, look and listen and pray with my ears, pray for an opening, a way out ...

Hillabee Hopper

"Know how you feel. I'm a hopper too," said a very big voice attached to a very small mouth belonging to a precocious nine-year-old tomboy with enormous eyes. "a master hopper. My name is Hillabee, Hillabee Hopper and I don't jump," she said, "not ever, not for any reason. Never two feet on the ground at once. Too long landings make me nervous. So, I keep my landings short. There are a lot of rules behind my carefree existence," she said, "My friends from the jungle have all tried to counsel me against such rigid rules but they are not to be trusted. Not being hoppers themselves they don't understand the importance of it. See, the bunnies are jumpers, the monkeys swingers and the frogs leapers. None of them hoppers," she said.

This seemed like a garbled wad of unintelligible yarn and I was fairly certain my wires had somehow gotten crossed with someone else's voices but I had never rejected a voice yet so thought it unwise to start now. Deep breath …

"I'll tell you their stupid advice later but here's what I think. Two feet implies commitment," she continued, "which means you don't have a choice. So, if you jump you give up your options and get stuck wherever you land. And who knows if its any good or maybe you get bored or maybe you just want to see what else is out there. All I know for sure is jumping is a catastrophic move resulting in sure disaster. Better to hop your way in and out of things, be a free operator.

"Now it's probably only fair to give you the advice of my jungle friends. We'll start with the queen of the bunny warren since her advice was at least partly in my favor. Now just so you know I usually talk with the regular bunnies but apparently she considered my uncompromising position on the hopping issue to be worth a visit, so about a week ago she stopped by. She was quite regal with her mini-tiara wrapped around the base of her long ears, until she opened her mouth and through her giant yellowy buck teeth came the raspiest voice I'd ever heard.

'A jump is really more like a two-footed hop,' said the Queen. 'The trick is in the balance.'

"I thought how terribly obvious, but you don't criticize the queen. So on she went."

'And hoppers have great balance what with all their rotating around on one foot. Problem is they can never relax and enjoy anything, so much shifting around all the time. Jumpers, on the other hand, get lazy because once they land they pay no attention to their center of gravity is. That is why my dear little Hillabee the trick is to jump without getting too comfortable,' she said scratching behind her very long ears before hopping off.

"So, it's really just like an elongated hop under the alias of being a jump. Why bother, I thought. And so what if she was the queen of the rabbit warren? Why did I have to change for her? And why does it seem everyone always wants me do what's right for them? What about what's right for me? I thought.

"And then there's the advice of my yippy teenage monkey friend who always shows up when I'm right in the middle of something and hangs upside down over my head yip yip yipping his head off. Take our conversation yesterday. I was explaining to him how I couldn't imagine ever settling down. Hopping was more than just an activity for me. It was a way of life.

'That's your banana junkie jivin' you,' the monkey told me.

"Pardon me," I said to him.

'Yeah, it's easy to jones when you get jacked on complacency,' said the Monkey as he swung down and landed almost on top of my feet. I stepped back. He stepped forward.

"You are in my space," I said.

'Then take it to the trees,' he replied

"But I'm not a monkey," I said.

'Don't need to be. But you can't hop up a trunk. If you don't commit to being there, you'll fall right out,' he said.

"He knew I'd always wanted to climb trees. I was just terrified of falling."

'Have to imagine it first,' he said. 'Just close your eyes and picture it and don't open your eyes till you have climbed the tree, jumped on a branch and are standing on two feet.'

"So I kept my eyes closed for a very long time and climbed until I got to that branch. The standing began feeling a two-footed landing and I panicked and fell out of the tree. When I opened my eyes I was still in my living room. Only now there was a bloated old freckled frog sitting on my coffee table staring at me with his big bulgy eyeballs.

"He stops by unannounced all the time. And boy, can he talk. He fancies himself a philosopher. So I'll tell you his advice but just so you know it gets a little twisty-turvy. So, good luck understanding him."

'Now what?' the frog said. 'You going to stumble around your head like a blood-drunk mosquito?'

"I stared at him, thinking perhaps he had had a few too many, but the whites of his eyeballs were clearer than a full winter moon."

'There are a lot of lily pads out there buddy,' he continued, 'and they look like a random mess of unrelated islands but there're a million paths. Just gotta jump your own. Think of it this way. Two-footed land, two-footed commitment—one to where you're jumping, the other to yourself.'

"I leaned back against the couch, dizzy from the swirling skirmish of such pond philosophy."

'The key to lily-pad landings is trusting that when it gets too sunny or shady or simply stops suiting you, there will be another,' he said

"So, it's the same as hopping." I said, smiling at the ultimate simplicity of it all.

'No.' he said. 'It is a series of jumps. You commit to each new pad wholeheartedly, eager for what it will offer you, where it may take you. But you also stay committed to where you ultimately want to go. So, if you end up not liking where your lily pad is floating to or it is sitting too still or it can't seem to find the sunlight or it is just a bad lily pad, you jump.'

"So you quit." I said.

'Yes.' he said. 'You quit being places that don't get you where you want to go. Because remember, one foot of the two-footed jump commitment is to you, your ultimate goal. Not like there's only going to be one lily pad for the rest of your life.'

"There was a long pause and I re-crossed my legs. He filled his miniature lungs or gills or whatever the hell they are with a giant breath. We sat in silence until a giant clap of thunder broke it. We both looked out the window—dry skies."

'You confused?' the frog asked.

"Not confused," I said. "Just don't really see the point. So what the hell's the difference between hopping and jumping if your commitment is that fickle?"

'The intention is not to quit but the priority is to commit to where you want to go,' he said.

"Same with hopping." I said.

'But without ever putting two feet down you can never truly know if you've landed where you want to be,' he said.

"I prefer defensive strategy. Not losing is a safer bet," I said triumphantly.

'What are you so afraid of losing?' he said.

"What?" I asked, stalling, hoping for some kind of a legit answer. Just then a large drop of rain hit the window followed moments later by a thousand others.

'When you quit something that is no longer working for you, what do you really lose?'

"Your commitment, your fight, your tenacity ..." I said not totally sure of what I was saying.

'Then hang on to that, if it works for you,' he said.

"The rain began pelting so hard it felt like a million knocks. It felt like the glass might crack, like the outside might come crashing in. "So, how do you know when to hop on?" I asked. He belched.

"Sorry, jump on," I corrected myself smiling.

'Never a sure thing,' he said. 'Just can't get distracted by fat mosquitoes or bigger pads. Gotta know your objective and stick to it,' he said

"And a few moments later he hopped off and I was left alone with a wet spot on my coffee table. To jump or not to jump ..."

Fear of loss—that was the obstacle.
What if it all fell apart?
What if I made a mistake I couldn't turn back from?
What if I commit to my biggest dream and it doesn't work out?
Then what?
And then I remembered that the myriad of things I have given up so far
have left me in the most beautiful place.

More or Less

I had hoped for more
more cocktail parties till 4am
with swirly glasses on very long stems
more wild laughter that spills over the edge
and simmers into what needs to be said.

I had hoped for more
more lusty conversation rings
'bout the deeper meaning of shallow things
more blustery autumn afternoons
and window-shopping beneath full moons.

I had hoped for more
but filled my life with less
somehow kept saying yes
to what in the end
has been the very best.

I had hoped for more
more Homeric odysseys
through foreign lands and stormy seas

more quiet walks through daisy fields
and naps that leave the spirit healed.

I had hoped for more
more Gatsby linen and flowing white
in T.S. Eliot's mocha brown nights
more Mozart mornings that fill the air
and steamy teas that melt my cares.

I had hoped for more
but filled my life with less
somehow kept saying yes
to what in the end
has been the very best.

So I suppose it's me I thank
for more or less
this unlikely success ... of a life.

I had hoped for more
but filled my life with less
somehow kept saying yes
to what in the end
has been the very best.

I Am a Sumo Wrestler Living Inside a Size 4 …

I will never be comfortable living with myself. So much fight inside so small a framework. I keep engaging in these elaborate what-if disaster scenarios. You've read several already. It's like locking door after door after ten-thousand doors to my future. And over the course of the past decade I would say I've locked at least that many doors to possible futures. Why? Because I always see the possibility for catastrophic failure. And by catastrophic failure I mean anything that isn't a raging success. Remember Mrs. Nardone's first grade class? Here's another little gem from that carefree time of innocence.

Got a paper back that had an A+ written on it. The girl next to me had an A+ written on her paper too but underneath in beautiful light blue script it read "Excellent." I tore my paper up, threw it on the floor and ran out of the room crying. Bit over the top? Well, sure if you don't care about perfection. It's a strange thing perfection. If it has to be perfect it is bound to be fail miserably because with goals set so high, the fall is like a gazillion stories. And I try to avoid tragic splattered landings.

What if I become famous and have a concert where I forget all my words? What if I am painfully off-key? What if I undersell the song and people get bored or leave or boo? What if I take a chance on my outfit and look like an overstuffed barmaid? Of course all this requires I actually finish the album and find someone to write music for it and rehearse a few times and find a venue to sing at, blah, blah, blah. It was exhausting.

Why couldn't my what-if scenarios center around questions like: What if my songs are so successful I feel heard in a way I never dreamed of? What if by giving my voice a stage I find happiness I never imagined? What if my songs touch millions of people and I feel deeply loved? What if singing them to my son creates a bond I never would have shared? What if believing in my dream makes me the kind of person that inspires the people around me? What if it makes my husband fall deeper in love with me? What if it makes me fall more in love with myself? And the world. And life? What if all these things are true?

But what if they're not and I fail miserably? That's what I always came back to. Doesn't matter how many times I've heard "you have to fail to succeed" or "you can be perfect or happy but not both." Doesn't matter. I seem committed to the idea of protecting myself from possible catastrophe. And it's ironic really (or maybe just painfully predictable) that the more I try to protect myself from failure, the more I get in the way of my success. The vulnerability of letting go, of saying good-bye to a way of thinking, a way of life that has kept me afloat (however far out to sea I may be) is daunting.

So once again I clear my mind of expectation and try to open it to whatever voice comes my way. I quiet and quiet and quiet until slowly this time after much waiting and some tears that need to exit with the fear I begin to hear, to listen …

Harmful Hannah

"Write a letter. And say good-bye. You know catastrophe and this isn't one. These are old fears hovering over a different present. Say good-bye. Bid them out. Now," said a girl hidden almost entirely in shadow but none the weaker for her lack of physical presence.

And for the first time the voice is familiar, hauntingly familiar. I have heard it before but from inside, not out. It feels safer somehow from this distance.

"I am not like the other girls so don't be alarmed. I am a ghost born the failed embryo of misguided love. I lived and died for you and would never have caused you such pain had I any idea I was. You were my world and so my story is inextricably tied to your own. The point of my story is that it is over. Its moral is as always in its ending, your beginning. Funny how they always go hand in hand." And in an uncomfortably even voice she introduced herself, "My name is Hannah, Harmful Hannah," she said.

"Festering incubation, late to hatch and I'm dead already. Good twelve year run-though. Pen, paper and a few well-placed words with real intention. Zap. Vaporized right into thin air," she said. "There were plenty of assassination attempts. Plenty. Five therapists, four social workers, three pharmacologists, two hospitalizations, plus reiki specialist, light therapist, bio-rhythm engineer, astrologist, psychic, past life regressionist, and, oh yes, the husband. Survived 'em all," she said.

This wasn't going to be observational, not like the rest. I could feel her in my gut and it hurt. I wanted to walk away but I didn't. With hands balled into fists I dug my nails into my palms in case I forgot where I was. I wasn't sure I wanted to go where I knew she was going.

"Little girls have shadows," she continued. "All of them do. I was hers. Adults are mirrors. Children too. It's how the light image takes hold. Her mom was perfect. Her dad was perfect. And so too, after a while, was everyone, small and large. But she was an imperfect little perfectionist. So she kept trying. Harder and harder and harder until trying became synonymous with failing and harder became easier because easier was a well-worn groove. The convoluted logic became muddy and she got stuck. And I was there.

"Solitude, too much, anchors shadows. My host had no friends. Her parents were very busy. So, she hung out in her closet and wrote love poems to me. I grew. And grew and grew, as did her belly. No one likes chubby girls. Chubby girls have bigger shadows but chocolate made her happy so I fed her pounds of chocolate everyday. She became pregnant with my darkness. And then the rape occurred. It glued us together. She remembered nothing except fear and pain. She clung fiercely. And I reigned supreme—the only familiar friend in her freakishly shifting world. She became my love-hostage and she loved me desperately, wickedly, crazily.

"We were inseparable until high school. Then came friends, popularity, humor and three years of estrangement. Seemed like an eternity. But she was in too deep and my hold too strong. And the rape would not be over for a very long time. And I knew she'd have to face it at some point so I just tried to help her along. I became the invisible man—the one she'd never seen. I would tap her on the shoulder with my cold, cold hands and disappear when she turned around. Her body froze. Her heart raced. Her memory reached out for pictures but there were none. No details. No handle. No one to hold on to but me. And we were back, stronger than ever.

"We spent days and nights together. She begged me for a way out, for some peace, any peace in this thunderstorm of memory. And I gave it to her. I showed her a better way, a way to release all the anxiety. And so began the porcelain purges. Fourteen years of love in the bathroom. And I helped her binge more so she could release more. And I let the "invisible man" and the "chubby girl" and the "imperfect little perfectionist" go away. For those few moments. They always came back. The more we purged the stronger they got. The terrible threesome.

"I taught her to hide. Others would seek. We hid behind charm and wit and talent. What pain? Where? We are perfect. Happy. Delighted to be here, please pass the ice cream. Just kidding. Just humor. And gradually the facade became facile. And there was almost no room for the pain, save for the porcelain trips.

They became frequent, sometimes six a day. Such traveling made her weary. She needed me more than ever. And I was becoming stronger than she was. I had begun to assume her identity. I had become a "we." She had become a "we". We had become an "us."

"Until our junior year abroad in England. Food was sparse. Bathrooms scarce. And control seemed to be slipping away. So I taught her to starve, taught her to strike against the very thing that caused her pain. And we did. And when we got hungry I reminded her food is for the weak, the needy, the emotional gluttons of the world. So we held out, stayed strong and lost pound after pound until she barely existed. And the less there was of her, the more of me. I had become her brain, her body, her heart. And we were almost one in the darkness, until the call. Souls can be so unpredictable. Unaffected by malnutrition or depression they reach out. She called her parents. They shipped her home. They celebrated Christmas. And we celebrated the unlimited food supply and private purging facilities. We were in love again.

"Then, back in Chicago, we got into laxatives. Eventually twenty at a time. She couldn't take the constant rumbling in her belly and the unpredictable explosiveness of it all. So, she committed herself to the hospital. For three months. And I waited, patiently. I knew it wouldn't last forever. And they could never love her the way I did. And I was right. Three months later we were back, but not the way we'd been—more distant, formal. It was awkward. I had to fight against the hospital hangover, the "healthy habits" they had tried to instill.

"I brought back the invisible man. I had to think of something new, more powerful. She had weapons she'd acquired to fight the cold, cold hands. So I went subconscious, went to the movies. It was my only shot at getting back the intimacy we'd had. I sent her to see *Cape Fear* with her boyfriend. The remake. She fell in love with DeNiro ... so charming, trustworthy, caring. She watched him adoringly turning paler with every bit of his betrayal. After it ended, the movie, she walked out with her boyfriend. He asked if she was okay. She said of course and quite suddenly started screaming and crying uncontrollably. He walked her outside. She walked sweater-less through the snow, refused to be touched or held or driven. She sobbed quietly, then violently in fits and starts, muttering in between how no one would hear to her. She didn't stop for hours except to get coated napkins from a gasoline station to blow her nose. He followed, begging her to get in the car. But I knew what he didn't. And before too much longer she had walked herself home and before too much longer I would be consoling her holding her blond head over that porcelain bowl. And it was over. For then.

"Shadows are longer in the winter but the snow reflects the light. This white winter lasted ten years. There was a marriage—less committed than ours, a career—less successful than ours and an abortion. I shared her with the husband and he was safe. For her. And me. We couldn't be pushed aside. Somehow, he knew.

"And then she found the mirror she'd been looking for all her life. There he was. In his eyes she saw the "her" she'd been looking for, the her that was silly, creative, passionate and deep. In him she saw her passion as eccentric not impractical, inspirational not cute. She felt vital, alive. And she came alive. She divorced her husband and kicked me out. I thought it was over. She'd found what she was looking for and it wasn't me. And he didn't last but she did. She forgot to be sick, forgot to feel sad, forgot the crime committed onto her. And I was sure we'd never see each other again.

"And then she remembered, remembered it all. Very slowly, it came back, harder this time. And she tried harder. And harder. And harder. But in the end she begged me back and begged me for something new, something more powerful to release the pain, something more tangible, more visible. And I handed her a knife. And she started cutting x's in her wrists. Why x's? She wouldn't say. I wondered if it was to ward off the memory. Or perhaps she was kissing the wound she'd never seen. And we threw them all together in a big boiling pot—starving, purging, cutting and doubt. But we talked less.

"She admitted herself again. The last hope check-in—this time to the fancy shmancy Menninger Clinic lock-down unit. Determined to exorcise it all, including me. No matter what. So, she befriended a bipolar newscaster who turned on her and got roomed with a manic-depressive who cried all day and night inconsolably. She got her daily individual therapy once a week and attended group with a couple of high-profile football rapists. Well, alleged rapists. They didn't act out. Or make too lewd remarks. Or engage in any noticeably abhorrent behavior. They just did their time and returned to their team. She needed a team. So, I got called back off the bench. Shortly thereafter we got sprung.

Shattered last hopes lead to death or faith. Fairly black-and-white. The former gives me power, control, life-saver status. The latter makes me a marionette. Times were tense.

"We moved back to New York. She moved in with a guy who loved her but couldn't reach her. And we kept the pot boiling, right over the edge sometimes. She had a shrink who loved her but couldn't reach her. We added smoking to the pot. She met another guy, the guy, the mirror that wouldn't crack. He loved her imperfections and she fell in love with his. Then she fell in love again. With a woman who brought her faith. They worked hard together for one year. And she began questioning my love, began re-evaluating what I contributed to her life. She decided her power was something she could no longer give away, not under any circumstance. And the Thanksgiving of her thirty-second year she broke it off.

"She let me live out back for a while just in case but I could feel it was over. And then came the first letter. I was heartbroken. She said we couldn't be together anymore—that she'd outgrown me and didn't need me, appreciated my being there, but had to say good-bye. And then one year later the second letter came—the one that returned my greatest gift, the knives, the cutting. And I knew. She said the x's had been her attempts to cross out the pain but she wasn't afraid of it anymore. She said we had to end for her life to really begin, that no matter how rough things got she would not give up. No matter how dark it got, she would never go back," she said.

And with that, the shadow that she had barely been through this painfully familiar story, disappeared entirely into the light. And I was left with overwhelming nausea from the gripping fear that had only recently become a memory. But there was also a sweeping sense of awe. And gratitude.

My what-if scenarios used to be about life and death—
sometimes literal, sometimes just the figurative question of whether I'd ever be
able
to really experience joy or pain or anything without my disorders surrounding
it.
So the idea that I had somehow evolved to a place
where what if involved hope and dreams and the opportunity to smile deeply
was nothing short of a miracle.

Hard to Find

Running into spring is sometimes …
not the easiest thing
my heart so heavy with wondering
fear of cold still lingering.

Docks step out to meet the sea
sunlight hovers over eternity
one bird on a wire, one boat for sale
that's all I need to get me by
one or two reasons, one or two signs
that hope won't be so hard to find.

Don't know why I'm so afraid
of getting through these longer days
just can't imagine more to do
taking on the heat of new.

Docks step out to meet the sea
sunlight hovers over eternity
one bird on a wire, one boat for sale
that's all I need to get me by

one or two reasons, one or two signs
that hope won't be so hard to find.

Stubborn snow
green green grow
hold on, don't go
just wait—I'll show you
some stuff I know.
Took a lifetime to figure out
I can be a little slow to start
but watch out baby cause when I do
ain't no stoppin' the things I do.

Docks step out to meet the sea
sunlight hovers over eternity
one bird on a wire, one boat for sale
that's all I need to get me by
one or two reasons, one or two signs
that hope won't be so hard to find.

I am a Dollhouse Wrapped in Plastic …

Play for me is a four letter word. It was growing up and the philosophy somehow stuck. If you are not accomplishing something, you are wasting time. As much as I occasionally, very occasionally try, I am afraid I will never feel safe to play.

I have disco danced in my living room to Earth, Wind and Fire, driven real fast in no real hurry and watched raindrops fall down the window for hours. But not often and certainly not lately. And truth is, I really don't have much experience having not really done it as a kid. So, it's easy to forget how. Anyway, there is always too much to do, too much left undone. There's contractor issues, family obligations, dogs that need shots, a baby that needs to be breast-fed. There is too much to do. And playing accomplishes none of it. In fact, playing produces absolutely nothing. In the end, it is a time-eating, money-grubbing leech, sucking away energy from important things that need getting done. I mean, how are you supposed to write an album skipping stones or sipping shakes or counting dandelions? Better to be doing something to make that dream come true. Doing was my theme and not just doing something but doing something productive. How else would it all get done? And the idea that maybe not everything had to get done was absurd, self-indulgent—practically sacrilegious.

It ate away at me though—this insidious, ascetic position. And I knew better but could never seem to get out of the way of myself. Playing felt somehow disrespectful to my dream, like I was ignoring it, turning my back on it. But always working my ass off made me feel like a worm rotting my red delicious dream from the inside out. And the harder I worked at saving it, the more I

63

seemed to poison it until finally I'd end up resenting the dream and hating apples altogether. It was a joyless way to be.

For a long time I blamed my parents for this obviously learned behavior. But in the end blame always falls backward. So, I'm trying to stop pointing to history, stop trying to retackle the origin of my neurosis and actually do something about it. My Mom had inherited it from her Mom who had inherited it from her Mom who had inherited it from her Mom … It went at least three generations deep and for all I knew we were all descended from Puritan stock. But being mostly Scottish, Irish and Swedish I couldn't quite figure it out. Course my mother did bring with her a smattering of German and English so very well could have been her ancestors. And their blood was probably far thicker. Didn't matter now though. The baton had been passed long enough. Time to hand off something different.

Luckily a few years back I got tricked into realizing that play is actually productive. I was working with my art director partner against a very tight deadline. We needed three campaigns. We had one and not a very good one. I was panicked. My partner decided we should go to Borders and listen to music. I told him he was crazy and we would do no such thing. This was no time to take a break. He said it was the perfect time. We were getting nowhere and he was going. I was welcome to join him. Completely against my better judgment but without feeling like there was no good alternative, I went. We listened. And I got introduced to Dave Mathews and found the soundtrack for *Breakfast Club* and bought my first Puccini opera. And we went back and came up with two brilliant campaigns. It was that easy. Walk away empty. Come back full. Creativity needed to be romanced, not bullied. So, I got it. But a lifetime of the opposite training and my very driven personality made it hard to hang on to.

Every now and then I am able to tap back into that genius and have the strength and will and passion to start my play-will-rule-the-day revolution, where I demand better treatment from myself, demand fair play, less pressure and a willingness to picket on these issues for longer than five minutes. My approach usually involved coercing someone, usually a sister into embarking on the adventure with me. It was a risky proposition, going in-family because we all came from the same Puritan place but the request came so rarely and our love ran so deep they were usually capable.

But lately I was finding I needed more and was less willing to lean so much on them. I could see a space carved out for me with a huge sandbox in it. If only I could just get my feet to walk in that direction and jump in—just once. I was sure I could repeat it and eventually treat it like I do my workouts, as non-negotiable activity necessary for overall well-being. If only I could make it to the sandbox.

And so I sat back wiggling my toes in imaginary sand and began to listen. I listened at first to the sound of sand falling through my fingers and then to the sound of children giggling and waves crashing and seagulls and then silence and then came the voice ...

Ella Weeeeeeez the Eccentric

"Playing is serious business. Nothing silly about silliness. In fact, I am rawther tired from all the scurrying to and fro. From the bawth to the couch to the frig and back. It is terribly exhausting. What do I care? I am Ella Weeeeeeeeeeeeeeeez," said a plucky little voice.

"There is much to be done. Must visit all the girls, drop off chocolates, sling mud—dirt if the water is too, too far away and get home in time to read a magazine and dash off a note to someone somewhere who must miss me terribly by this point," she said jetting around in a veritable flurry of activity.

"I have three hats. Sometimes I wear them all together but not usually. There's Eraserhead, the reversible gray and black fleece hat. I wear her when the weather is frightfully bad and getting worse. There is Runaway Runway, the oversized reversible black-on-black hat. She is very lovely and can only be worn on short car trips to important events of two or more diplomats or movie stars. Can't be raining or snowing and especially not sleeting. Lastly there is Stripey. He is not so much a hat as a fleece ear band I wear when I don't want to listen to anyone else for goodness sake."

She was charming, precociously, delightfully charming and I smiled inside and out as I listened to her liltingly, lovely silliness.

"Turtle Fur, they are my slippers. Blue outside and red in. Of course, they're not real turtle fur. Turtles don't have fur. They go on immediately after all bawths and before bedtime rubbing and during any bouts of exhaustion or chocolate droughts or when my feet get miserably cold. They are not allowed outside, not under any conditions, not even in the spring to pet bunnies on the nice green grass. That is a NO!

"Crunchy Cookie are my brown clogs. They have a gray racing stripe around the top and last year I wore them every day except to black tie affairs and the gym. They are always ready to go and don't have any silly ties or laces or other such shoe drama. I love Crunchy Cookie.

"Brown Bear is my uniform. I wear it everywhere. To the movies and the store, out for frozen yogurt and shopping on the Champs Elysées which I do twice a week to keep all my freckles from getting bored. It's not easy and we have no budget but there's quite a lot to see. Mon dieu! Every week or two Brown Bear gets washed. I do an elaborate sudsy water dance in my knickers and T-shirt. The music is in my head and I turn it up very loud. Then when they have to go in the dryer, I light cranberry candles to protect them against the maniacal shrink demons. When they come out I put them on immediately and run right out to celebrate.

"Plants don't make it here. Not any race of plant. No idea why either. There was Frank the Topiary who we bought in the summer. He lost all three of his big fat green bellies slowly throughout the fall. By December he was practically naked. And anyone who knows anything knows you can't put a naked plant out on the terrace in the blizzardy brrrrr of winter. And we couldn't take him to plant heaven so close to the holidays so Frank eventually turned into a collection of branches we hung dish towels on to dry.

"I live with the Tartans and Cecelia and Cecil. The Tartans spend all day in bed. They aren't sick. They are undercover secret agent twin bears with little tartan plaid vests. One of them has a matty spot on his forehead where he was kissed by an angel. They both have big bellies that stick out under their vests. They get milk and cookies along with special secret agent messages from a winged monkey that delivers it all at 3:00 P.M. every day. I am not allowed to be present for these visits, not under any conditions. That is another NO!

"Cecelia and Cecil just moved in. Cecelia is a winged bear angel who carries her best buddy frog friend, Cecil everywhere. They came to visit Christmas morning and stayed. They get along with the Tartans just fine although they do not approve of secrets. Not one little bit.

"The Monkey and the Devil hang downstairs. They sit right across from each other on opposite walls but they never speak. Don't even acknowledge each other's existence. They each have their own teeeeribleeeeeeeeeeee important agenda. The Devil is green from drinking too much absinthe. He is in charge of stirring up big amounts of trouble and then freezing when anyone looks at

67

him as if he's just some picture on the wall. The Monkey on the other hand drinks some kind of aperitif. That's it. It's a purely liquid diet. He has an incredibly lot of stories cause he's been alive for over a century but don't ask. They are long, long, long and no one lives happily ever after.

"There are also two bunnies and a rabbit. They are not related. Annie ran away from a frightfully stuffy antique store. She is a very proper misfit with ears taller than her body and legs longer than her ears. She doesn't crouch or jump but rather leans philosophically. Blue Bunny on the other hand is a croucher. He is furry and blue and swallowed a jingle when he was little so when you press his belly it sings. The Rabbit, known to his friends as the Rabbit, has even more enormous ears than Annie. He is made of brass and holds a small round tray in his paws. Only the keys to his kingdom can go there. He is even more trouble than the Devil and Monkey together … Oh my!

"Two things you should know before I go—sneezing and hiccups. Wasn't built for either. And there is nothing normal about either one. A double 'oh my' if you ever hear them together or back-to-back. My sneezes were designed by the guy Mother Nature hired to invent the hurricane. Not subtle. They demand all passers by say *gobleshuuuu!,* which they mostly do. My hiccups are schizophrenic, like swallowed burps hog-tying exhaled air bubbles. It is bizarrely frog-like with the rib going in and bits coming out. Luckily neither happens too terribly often unless I am sick, nervous or inhaling too much oxygen. Gotta run. Much to do," she quipped flitting off to some other pressing engagement.

Oh to be that fanciful and free …
I wondered what it would take, what it would mean
to lose the fear, let go of the drive,
figure out how to embrace the joy of being alive.

What Would it Mean

Softer, softer, softer still

need shelter from this mountainous hill

that started as a pleasure dome

decreed the mighty Kubla Khan

but morphed beneath my steely will

to ice and frost and bony chill.

Just what would it mean to let it all go

to slowly exhale a long breathy trail … of fears

to let injustices stand,

let anger sift like sand,

hold joy in the palm of your hand.

It's nothing radical or new,

nothing revolutionary,

just so hard to do.

Tomorrow will be what tomorrow will be

and all the planning in China won't make the tea.

Been steeping in this world of what-if's

but thirsting for something not so stiff.

Keep holding on tighter to railings of hope

railings of mirrors, mirrors and smoke.

And I wonder just what would it mean to let it all go

to slowly exhale a long breathy trail … of fears

to let injustices stand,
let anger sift like sand,
hold joy in the palm of your hand.
It's nothing radical or new,
nothing revolutionary,
just so hard to do.

Cause there's this evil seed inside my dreams
driving me to obscene extremes
and in the taming of my vision
lost sight of what's been given.
Can't seem to find the inspiration
get past these broken expectations.

Just what would it mean to let it all go
to slowly exhale a long breathy trail … of fears
to let injustices stand,
let anger sift like sand,
hold joy in the palm of your hand.
It's nothing radical or new,
nothing revolutionary,
just so hard to do.

I am a Zen Master Tripping
Over Boulders of Thought ...

I think every little thing to death and it nearly kills me. I can take any issue and break it down into its' every single molecular proton. And then as I study each infitesimal blip under a microscope I wonder why I seem unable to see the bigger picture. Overprocessing the ittiest bittiest detail, that is my specialty. And there is barely a detail of my life that doesn't get thought to death. It's not that most details aren't worthy of sincere consideration—just not over-the-top obsession.

Crackdown in Danbury on Illegal Immigrants. There was a time this was just a headline, a headline that evoked mixed emotion. Post-9/11, send them home. Shouldn't be here if they're not legal. This would be mixed with remorse since no one in this country, save the Indians would be living here if it not for immigrants. It's our foundation, our bedrock, our history. So, who are we to deny others from making it theirs? It would have been a moral, philosophical question. Never would have occurred to me to wonder who, what individuals, what were their names, their stories. Did they have kids? How long were they here? But now we have a Brazilian nanny named Janette, who our little boy loves, who sings beautiful songs in Portuguese to him, who works harder than I ever have, who is loyal, kind, lovely and illegal, living in Danbury.

So philosophical becomes personal and spins a thousand webs in my brain. How can we make her legal? How many attorneys do we know? Will there be another period of amnesty? Should we consider forging documents? Will we go to jail for it? Can we sponsor her? Can we afford it? Will she stay? What guarantees do we have? Are there ever any? What guarantees do we have our house construction will finish on time? And where will we go when our rental runs out? And what more can we do to eek all these things along there way

71

toward some semblance of order. And that is how it starts out as one thing and then spirals into a web of similarly themed issues. How on earth can we begin resolving one when there is a line a mile long of others? And how do you determine which is most important? And how do you resolve to resolve anything?

This is always how it starts—in search of resolution. But the number of questions and sub-stratospheres of three-dimensional answers, each with its own hemisphere of variables makes arriving at the sought-after resolution impossible. And so I spin around in my constellation of fears, hopes, doubts, goals—spinning and spinning and spinning until eventually I begin to spiral down and the force-field is no longer my own but the black hole of doom I have somehow created.

Sometimes it gets sparked by the silliest things, things I would never have imagined. And they end up taking me down precarious, treacherous trains of thought. For example, two weeks ago I was jogging by a big old colonial a few streets over on Birch. It was getting a facelift and out front were three masons standing in front of very large stones. With what looked like widgets they were picking away at these monster stones in hopes of creating smaller ones. I measured the length of the front yard in my mind, looked at the number of boulder-like stones and laughed. Never in a million years was this stone wall ever going to get built, I thought. They are the slowest workers I've ever seen and they'd need about fifty fast workers to make any noticeable progress anyway. Plus, it was hard to believe there wasn't a more advanced stone-working tool than the widget. Doesn't matter though because the contractor probably won't pay them and they'll walk off the job and these people will get stuck with a bunch of loose stones.

And then it got personal. The stone wall turned into an obvious sign from the universe that our house would never be done and we'd become bankrupt trying to finish it and unable to get a certificate of occupancy we'd have to foreclose on it. And blah, blah, blah—the trail into darkness—all on this gorgeously sunny day.

Here's the twist. Today I jogged by the stone wall again. And it is almost finished. And it looks absolutely gorgeous, one of the finest I've seen. The same three masons were placing stones right up to the leveling string in their sweat-soaked T-shirts. Perhaps this was a sign to ignore the other sign. I got conflicting signs like this all the time that were not so much signs really as they were excuses to run headfirst in a direction without assessing whether it was, in the end, a dead end. And I knew in my heart somehow, and maybe not the way I thought, that the house would come together and Janette would be okay and life would go on its merry little way regardless of my insanity.

And so wouldn't it be brilliant to lose the insanity and embrace all the unfinished stone walls out there—to remember with everything, it won't look like any of it will come together until it has—and to remember, and this last part I knew would be hard—that it's not such a long way from widgets to walls.

And so I would have to listen for these reminders even when they were a long way from my racing mind. And so again as I have done many times now, I listened, listened in the hope of better understanding how to listen and sure enough I heard ...

Thandie the Thinker

"Easier said than done," said a most calming voice. "But well worth the effort. My name is Thandie, Thandie the Thinker. My overthrow three years ago left me dumbfounded. I was queen commander-in-chief of all the girls for twenty years. Campaigned for the first ten. Reigned for twenty. And then slowly over the course of about three years everything began to disintegrate. Would have been easier if they'd just confiscated my crown, cut the legs off my throne and painted my gray palace pink. But it didn't go down like that.

"The campaigning years were a bitch. The girls were fresh. I was fresh. And I knew if I didn't get them into a group and reason them into my camp early on I'd be dead. Problem was every time I seemed to have them all together listening attentively, backs to the wall another girl would crop up somewhere over the horizon and in order to get her I'd have to leave the others alone. By the time I'd get back they'd be everywhere wandering the hills, picking wildflowers, making mud baths for stray frogs, counting clover leaves … you name it. So, I'd go through the same rigmarole all over again. Few girls were reasonable so I found the weight of mass opinion and constant mental gymnastics to be the brutal force I needed to bully them into my camp.

"To be clear, not all was hunky dory back at camp. There were rebels and runaways. The free spirits and creative ones were huge flight risks and the bleeding hearts were willing to fall on their sword for any emotional cause. And in retrospect I think my ultimate downfall was in not letting the outcasts out, not banishing them from my kingdom without worry. But at that time I was afraid they'd be able to amass their own troops and take me over which is of course exactly what they did—from the inside. Shortsighted of me I know.

"Unfortunately, even for a thinking leader and a leading thinker, my strategy always seemed in survival mode, always in crisis control so there was never a long game, never a chess like approach to my rule. My ambition was matched move for move by impatience. Foreign policy was based solely on defense and domestic affairs were run with band-aids and tunicates. I forced the poets into a metronome, stuck the bleeding hearts into a pushpin ball and crammed the

free spirits into a four-by-four—whatever it took to ma
beyond a shadow of a doubt sure that I was in total contr
wise, dealing with the so-called diplomats from the country ،
island of family and the continent of friends would be absolut،   ،y
impossible.

"Besides even these three superpowers, there were all kinds of rogue lone shooters and random third-world threats like identity thieves and collection agencies, flat tires and rip-off mechanics, off-sale merchandise and imposing budgets. There were hundreds of these additional skirmishes, plenty of which led to battle and a good number of which came completely out of the blue. No ability to plan, strategize or allot energy toward the right resources (although I was rarely sure of what those would be). Since the bleeding-heart constituents were not on my side voluntarily, I couldn't count on them to subside the panic such attacks brought on.

"Finally, the teeth-chattering fear of imminent overthrow eventually began affecting my dental health, resulting before long in five impacted teeth. The jaw aches were excruciating. So, finally the dentist removed them all and replaced them each with tiny ivory fortresses welded to my gums in steel. Hot and cold became intolerable, unbearable. Even warm and cool were too much. And so the steel had sealed the deal on my lukewarm experience of culinary delights. No ice cream or warm chocolate chip cookies. No soup or coffee or cold glasses of white wine. Everything was in between somewhere and nowhere. Mine became a room-temperature existence. Even the panic attacks were better than the boredom of fragile living. And it continued on like this where the nonessential, non-imperative things, the things lacking in a func-tional reason for being began to disappear. I developed severe sneezing aller-gies and the gardeners were instructed to behead my beloved tulips. I began having furious scratching fits and it was determined my dogs would have to be relocated.

"My paranoia escalated. It seemed impossible for my body to be failing me on such a mass scale and with such nonsensical will. It had to be something in my food or drink or perhaps fumes being sprayed in my sleep. Someone was behind it. And so I began sending the most likely culprits to criminal labor camps where they were charged with finding cures for my increasing ailments. Within months, everyone was suspect—the gardener, the cook, the chauffeur. But my deterioration continued. So, I began listening through the walls and slowly I began to hear voices. They were mere whispers at first but before long they were yelling. They yelled loudly inaudible things that I could not understand and my translators couldn't hear anything and so there was not even a loose interpretation. And the voices were so very loud but I was terrified if I didn't listen I might miss the message about the assassination attempt. And finally the voices got so loud I could tolerate no other noise at all—not music, not church bells, not even the sound of birds all of whom I was forced to exile to the southern part of the kingdom," she said pausing to catch her breath.

It was a Shakespearian tragedy, I thought. What could possibly be her point? I really hoped there'd be one.

"And as I lay in my de-downed, carpet-less, blacked-out window of a bedroom," she continued, "they came to me one by one and said good-bye. Assassination was upon me. I could feel it. And I no longer really cared. They told me I'd officially lost my mind and asked if I was ready to let it go. I said yes. Beheading seemed fitting.

"The first day before sentencing I heard nonstop ringing. It had the most piercingly cosmic tone like mortality was calling, karma stopping by, the Boogie Man waking me up. It sounded like the steady monotonous dinging of my failures being measured out or the hourly tolling of church bells passing judgment as they took away time.

"The second day before sentencing I heard the distinct sound of cage rattling. Each rattle sounded remarkably like the end of innocence, like the last time the last toy on earth would be shook and at the same time like a country trapped behind rusty bars trying to taste freedom.

"The third day before sentencing I heard the reverberation of a thousand barely pinpointable echoes, like a long looped list of don't forget to do, didn't mean to say, must pay, need to visit, should really write down, owe a thank-you, call-back, apology. It started before I woke up and played throughout the day going double-speed before bed. It was like a string of audible rosary beads slowly strangling me with their broken promises.

And then came the sentencing. Apparently my dream trilogy had healed me of the three diseases responsible for infecting my thoughts and making me lose my mind. So, I was not beheaded. I was sentenced to a life free of thought. I was sentenced to a life making daisy chain necklaces for children by the sea. Because only by the sea does the ringing and cage rattling and reverb cease to be. Only there, can you hear the waves laughing and the children's feet crashing on the shore as seagulls race their shadows along the beach. There, there are only the breath holes of crabs as the tide rolls out, the millions of shiny wet stones waving the ocean in. And with each wave of inspiration I became the water and within minutes I could feel all that swims within me. It was magical. Here I was found."

So it was about trading in the thoughts and the worry and the drama
for simple pleasures.
It was about getting back to what mattered,
remembering where joy came from and focusing there.
To be free from thought
and full of faith.

Unfolding Faith

Unfolding faith, unfolding faith
like blankets before bed
side to side and end to end
over and over again.
Unfolding faith, unfolding faith
like dreams upon their dawn
hungry for translation
the forward-moving pawns.

Go back, go back, go back
to your lovers hands,
your child's feet.
Go back, go back, go back
and hold on tighter
to how you feed
your tired and hungry soul.
Yes, hold on, hold on tighter
to how you feed your soul.

Unfolding faith, unfolding faith
like paper from your pocket
what's inside, what could be
the endless curiousity.

Unfolding faith, unfolding faith
like letters from a fire
looking to decipher
what's inside desire.

Go back, go back, go back
to your lovers hands,
your child's feet.
Go back, go back, go back
and hold on tighter
to how you feed
your tired and hungry soul.
Yes, hold on, hold on tighter
to how you feed your soul.

I interviewed religion,
toyed with philosophy,
played around with nothingness,
tried to find my inner bliss
and after all my searching,
this is what I found
love and truth and poetry is where it's at for me
and energy, our energy
don't see how this could cease to be.
Yeah, love and truth and poetry is where it's at for me
and energy, our energy
don't see how this could cease to be.

So, go back, go back, go back
to your lovers hands,
your child's feet.
Go back, go back, go back

and hold on tighter
to how you feed
your tired and hungry soul.
Yes, hold on, hold on tighter
to how you feed your soul.

I am a V-8 Stuck Inside a
Horse and Buggy ...

Big plans. Lots of energy. And yet seems like I'll never make it where I want to go. Never make it anywhere exciting. Seems like I always get stuck in between. I have all the energy in the world to move forward but there keep being new obstacles that get thrown in my way. So I spin my wheels faster and faster and faster until I am so deep in my own rut I just have to cry. And it helps. I spend most of my time trying to be upbeat and positive and look on the bright side, so crying helps. It is exhausting, totally and completing exhausting, but good.

Take the extra eight pounds around my middle. I had to wait six weeks after my delivery to do anything physical. Fine. I waited, even though there was no question in my mind as soon as the Morphine and Percoset and extra strength Motrin wore off I could get out there and do it. Just like the commercial. I wouldn't let a little C-section get in my way. Unfortunately, the whole getting up out of a chair was a bit harder on my belly than I had predicted. This was insanely disappointing, considering how hard I worked on my pre-pregnancy abs in hopes of making this aftermath easier. But okay. So, it would not happen week three. Or four. End of week five I'd had it. Couldn't take any more sitting around. So, I got myself out there and went for a nice little jog. Four miles seemed aggressive but reasonable given my great pre-pregnancy shape. Wrong. The pain around my incision and muscles after was unpleasant, very.

But nothing short of a hospitalization would stop me from trying again in a few days. Plus, my six-week check-up was only two days away. Even I could wait that long. It wasn't so much about needing my body back, although buttoning—forget that—just zippering any of my jeans would have been nice. And it wasn't about the endorphin high although a rush of something besides breast milk wouldn't have been terrible. It was more that I needed not to be in-between the old me and the new me anymore. I needed to arrive at the new me, have a quick little welcomes party and move on. It didn't seem like an awful lot to ask. I had been patient, mostly. I hadn't bitched about anything during my pregnancy—not the complete and total lack of wine, sushi or soft yummy cheeses, not the constant peeing or back-pain or answering the same questions ten thousand times. I had been a veritable joy. Trust me.

And it wasn't that I wasn't happy now. I am happy. There's just this pervasive feeling of being unfinished—unfinished with the house, with deciding about work, with finishing my album and finally shedding these last eight pounds. I'd spent a good amount of time obsessing about the first items. No success. So, it seemed easier to focus on the eight. No contractors. No housewife fears or writer's blocks. Just pudge. I had fought it before. I could fight it again. Just be a hell of a lot easier if I could do some form of physical exercise.

A-okay. That was the doc's verdict. Do whatever you want. You are a fast healer and the incision is doing beautifully. Great. First, because there was almost no greater compliment than telling me that I was doing anything fast. And second, I hadn't done any real damage with my premature exercise. So, excellent. I would get back out there the next day, run my little heart out and not worry. And just for kicks and some hope of fitting back into my jeans I'd follow up my four miles with a good old set of crunches. But I'd be careful. Nothing too, too strenuous. Plan was a terrific failure. Cramps, pain, sore-ness—the works—and not in that good no pain/no gain way. Thwarted again.

I was beginning to feel like the roadrunner character. Except none of it was very funny. This is what was going to break me, these stupid eight pounds. I'd refer to them from the institution as the Final Fated Eight or the Eight that made me Break and who knows what other stupid fatalist bullshit I'd make up. The circumstance would be dire. And eventually I'd have to make up some other reason why I was there since weight loss wasn't all that interesting or tragic or worthy of insanity.

Anyway, here I am at week eight. No real change. I keep trying to "just do it" and end up regretting it. Not trying doesn't seem like a terribly pro-active decision. Cutting back to one meal a day seems a bit extreme. But something is going to have to give. I can't keep living in limbo.

And so I would again sit quietly and comfortably in my leather chair, back against my gray chenille pillow and listen and try to let go of the feeling I should be doing something more active and try to remember that listening was the very best and ironically most active thing I could do. And slowly my body settled in and my mind quieted and I listened and I listened and I heard ...

Sonya and Tonya the Twins

"Pleeeeeeeeease stop starting. Please just stop all this starting. Sometimes you just have to lay down, close your eyes and stop all this swooshing about," said a voice. "I am Tonya and she's Sonya," said Tonya gesturing at her compatriot. "We are the sick and tired twins," Tonya continued, "and we are positively, absolutely exhausted …"

"… and quite likely on the verge of a cold," picked up Sonya. "This whole 'starting' thing you seem hell bent on is making us work triple time," she wheezed.

"Would be easier if you'd just call it something else," mumbled Tonya, yawning. "Doesn't even matter what. Just trick us all into thinking it is a little game, make-believe, play time—anything but the beginning."

"Starting, beginning, initiating," Sonya said, "all of it leads to schedules and agendas and nearly immediate disappointment that more is not being done which means yet more beginnings. So, before we go any further we beg of you to please, pleeeeeease play, experiment, imagine but stop all this beginning. The pressure is too, tooooo much," she finished with a sigh and a slouch.

They were right, sure, but I wondered if there would be some kind of plan in this un-plan plan to resolve the jean issue. I'd wait and see.

"Anyway," Tonya said, "enough about you. Back to us. The other girls call us 'Sick and Tired' because we are always one or the other and quite frequently both. For example, right now we have pretty much nothing to say because we are … sick and tired. Feel like napping or vegging out to the Jewelry Channel or skimming spa getaway reviews or cellulite removal ads—anything that might improve our current state of exhaustion without actually having to do anything. I mean just breathing alone requires the coordination of thousands of molecules and brain waves and lung expansion and stomach rising and falling. It's a miracle we keep doing it. No idea how the other girls do," she said.

"'Doing, in general, you should know," said Sonya "is one of our very least favorite things. We are the ones who hide the To-Do list, encourage ample use of the snooze button and fully support the cancellation of any and all plans. Nothing is that paramount that it can't at the very least be postponed. Funny thing is we have no real home (too tired to look in the paper; too sick to call a broker) so we visit the other girls. We never stay more than a week, usually only a couple days and sometimes only a few hours but they always think we're moving in, never going to leave."

"Could be our seven eighteenth-century trunks, twelve hanging bags and twenty-two handbags," explained Tonya. "They never know where to put it all. Front hall is fine with us. But they hem and haw and get all snooty about it blocking the way, being burdensome for other visitors. Thing is, there are none, not while we're there. We tend to be a bit overwhelming. Luckily we are consummate guests and primo entertainers. We have at least four group naps, three independent ones and five to six bon-bon breaks."

"Ironically," Sonya added, "we really only wear the same couple of outfits. Coordinating takes such energy and then there's all the planning about what kind of a look and does the current weight situation permit it. Easier to go drawstring and sweatshirt or dressed up moo moo. Unfortunately, all choices seem to get a bit drafty. In fact, seems like we're on the verge of getting a cold now. Everyone always says, 'Oh my, well make sure you take Echinacea and lots of C."

"A hundred Prozac and a suitcase full of unmarked bills might be more to the point. Holistic vitamin prescriptions would mean my sickness was bacterial, viral, germy or deeply psychotic. Fact is that's usually not the half of it. There are almost twice as many other kinds. For example, there's the mental duress of enduring intolerably cheery pep talks, the chronic low-grade malaise result-ing from sugar lows and compulsive introspection and the demoralizing energy sap of differing opinions. It goes on and on. I feel quite under the weather and need now to retire to the tub," said Sonya.

"Yawn, yawn. All her moaning makes me exhausted. Blah di blah blah blu," said Tonya. "I am absolutely positively barely able to even get out the next few words I am so completely and totally wiped out. I am tired all the time. Sleeping makes me tired. Waking up makes me even more tired. The other girls keep me out till tortuous hours, get me up at ungodly hours and demand conscious activity for entirely too many hours. My eyelids are a gatrillion pounds and my brain is sinking in quicksand. Must go."

*It was confusing, the idea of doing nothing to get from A all the way to Z
but if I was honest with myself, which I don't usually like to be,
there was only so much I could do. Sometimes it wasn't about reaching any
higher.
It was about trusting in the way life unfolds, doing my best and
leaving the rest up to the day.*

Rolled-up Note in a Jelly Jar

So here I sit on the ground again hoping for some kind of sign
Clap of thunder, shooting star
rolled up note in a jelly jar
something more than yellow lights and worn-out souls
fogged up windows and two-way tolls
hoping for some kind of hold
on where it is I'm supposed to go.

Cuz' I'm flying below altitude again
under the radar, over the pain
trying to make sense of the clouds terrain
I keep reaching higher tryin' to make amends,
keep reachin' higher to see the end
but reachin' higher only gets me halfway.
The rest is up to the day ...
the rest is up to the day ...

So I sit on my way from A to B
lookin' for bridges to get me to Z
but all I can see are the ghosts in my mind
telling me wait for a better time,
sayin' honey you ain't the travelin' kind

so I'm lost on a byway that's run out on its name,
headed for somewhere I've never been.

And I'm flying below altitude again
under the radar, over the pain
trying to make sense of the clouds terrain
I keep reaching higher tryin' to make amends,
keep reachin' higher to see the end
but reachin' higher only gets me halfway.
The rest is up to the day ...
the rest is up to the day ...

I keep looking forward moving back
can't figure out why I'm so off-track
how my big ole' plans got so out of whack
but next time I'm leavin' the map at home
navigate new opinion zones.

Next time I'm letting go
and getting in the flow
leaving it up to the day
whatever it brings my way.

I am a Fuzzy Wooby
Encrusted in Ice …

It's not that I don't have mothering instincts because, although on a really bad day I can be just the slightest bit ice-princessy, the reality is I have strong mothering instincts toward my son. Just not toward myself. Strange, really that mothering him would be such a dream and mothering myself such a nightmare. There's just something about being warm and fuzzy with myself that feels self-indulgent and absurd. In fact, unless you're running a nursery school or animal shelter mothering seems to be viewed as kind of weak and wimpy in general. Never worked for me as far back as elementary school. My mild-mannered days (hard to believe there really were any) bring back memories of scratch fights and hair-pulling.

But over the next ten or so years I figured it out. Warmth is met with a cool reception and cool ironically is received quite warmly. So, I cooled off my approach. Sarcasm makes people laugh. Wit keeps people's attention. And cool keeps them coming back for more. Warm never got me invited to fun dinner parties. Never helped me negotiate better salaries. In fact, mostly it got me an earful of other people's problems. So, it was not on my list of desired qualities. Sweet and nice translated to boring and uninteresting. I was a good adapter.

Plus, warm didn't feel terribly realistic. The world wasn't warm. More appropriate to have a dark sense of humor about things since that was usually the nature of them. Only caveat was the darker and more cutting I got, the more scraped-up I got inside. Hard to separate outside from in. So, I would have to find some way of staying soft while still keeping my edge.

But I always associated soft with nurturing, caring, mothering. And being a mother (son being the miraculous exception) was never terribly interesting to me. In fact, I flat-out refused the role in my first marriage. No kids, no thank you. And until oh, about a year ago, I was pretty sure I would never sign up for it. Mothering always seemed like more of a series of obstacles and milestones, something for women looking to attend PTA meetings and play groups. It wasn't personal. It just wasn't for me. Seemed like a very, very long show from which you couldn't go home early no matter how tedious or boring or downright deplorable it got. It was something to be endured more than enjoyed. Plus, mothers were rarely songwriters or so I thought. Mothering would surely take me away from my writing, my life, myself. And I wasn't willing to give it all up.

Giving and giving up: that's what I thought loving mothering was all about. Sacrifice. You give up some of your dreams, some of your freedom, some of yourself. You give these things up in order for someone else to have them. It's a crazy generous proposition if you do it right. If you do it wrong you're a bitchy, selfish witch whose kids end up in financially crushing therapy and resent you forever. I didn't think I was generous enough for the first … or second so decided to opt out altogether. I mean I wasn't even good at being generous with myself.

And yet, sitting here now, eight-week-old baby in my arms, something has softened just the littlest bit. The sarcasm is not gone. Nor the dark humor. It's nothing I've had to give up so much as something I'm finally able to give in too. I am giving in to warmth, allowing myself to melt into it and it is different than I ever imagined. It is not a weakening but more like a strengthening, kind of the way rock, under extreme temperature, can melt and take new shape and become actually stronger through the softening than it was before. Or to make a metaphor closer to home, it's not like giving away a piece of pie and having that piece missing. It's more like working out, where expending energy leaves you with more.

So, I finally get that part. But once again it is about mothering another, not myself. So, I try to take the principles and reapply but it never seems to stick because somehow the mothering of self seems (even though I know it's an illusion) to be in direct conflict with mothering of other. For instance I can either spend an hour writing or breast-feed my son. Me or him. And that's where I get screwed up. Same logic applies to work, to house management, to family obligations, etc. I can't seem to fully grasp on any kind of an ongoing basis the idea that giving doesn't have to negate taking. I need to take in order to give. Taking is not the evil enemy stepchild. And giving alone is a crooked lie. Without feeding my head I can't nourish anyone else's. Not really. And when I give away pieces of myself without replenishing them I resent having given them at all. And since giving them away was my idea, I get to be responsible for robbing myself. Hmmm.

Doesn't feel like the brightest decision-making and yet I do it again and again. And the farther I get away from mothering from myself, from doing what feels good to me the more I forget what that even is and so the less I am likely to do it. And it doesn't help that no one really wants you to do it because of course they need what they need and the bigger picture story of they'd get more if they let me give to myself is only for the highly, highly evolved at the top of their game. And who of us really are?

So, mothering on a regular basis … taking charge of setting boundaries and not being bulldozed by pushy passive aggressive people … knowing when to say when and not falling prey to the martyr approach … not degrading into irresponsible self-mothering out of laziness … and not giving a shit about other peoples judging my behavior as selfish—these were the things I was hoping to get better at keeping top of mind. Nothing too complicated.

Again I began to listen but I listened this time not so much through my ears as through my heart knowing somehow that I was needed to listen in a way I hadn't before, to listen in a way that other people's voices could not infiltrate. And so I listened through the soft spongy membranes of my heart and it was blurry at first and then quiet but clear …

Wanda the Warrior

"Listen to nothing. Nothing," whispered the voice, "but your own voice."

She sounded so authoritative for so soft a voice and she looked unlike any of the other girls so far. Her image was made of a thousand reverberating echoes, a million vibrating forward-facing parenthesis. I recognized her from somewhere deep inside. She was familiar and yet somehow different than I remembered, like Hannah and yet not. I closed my ears and tried to listen.

"I am a frog hopping from lily pad to lily pad, from green to green on a sea of blue.

I am a rabbit hopping in and out of holes, no pocket watch, no Alice just late, late, late.

I am a monkey swinging from branch to branch, hanging upside down by my tail.

I am Wanda the Warrior," she said, "and I am not free, except in her imagination. I am her inner voice, her instinct."

I could feel her reverberation inside me. Could feel her feeling me. And somehow it seemed like we were one, like the "her" she spoke of was me.

Wanda continued. "I belong to her and she belongs to the queen and we are all at war. I am a prisoner of war," she said practically at a whisper.

So it was another internal war. I was the 'her' or 'she'. The Queen I wasn't sure about—perhaps my evil inner stepmother. And Wanda was my inner voice. I wasn't sure why she wasn't more direct, why she just didn't just refer to me directly. It would have been a lot less confusing but perhaps it is easier to hear a story without being responsible for it all and so again I listened.

Wanda continued again, faster, now having sensed my understanding, "I am locked in a stone cellar with no light save for the infrequent visits where she checks to make sure I haven't impaled myself against the wall or used my wily ways to work out some tricky treacherous plan. When she does check she removes only one rock. A single piercing ray of light nearly blinds me with hope, and it is dark again. The king and queen of the castle know nothing of my plight. Though if they did they would most certainly appreciate her keeping me removed from castle quarters. Unparliamentary-like behavior is frowned upon. For flat-out rebellion you can be iced right out of existence.

"So, finally around five I willed fire from my eyes and pierced right through the rocks. And for five years I was homeless, not long enough to work out some crazy hairstyle and slur of belligerent obscenities but long enough to know it gets cold in the winter and some places the winter lasts all year. I crawled back on frostbitten hands and begged.

"She chopped off my arms, cut out my vocal cords and put me on a yellow stretch school bus that made a never-ending loop around some far western suburb. I sat in the far back of the bus, in the jumper seat behind the regular ones. Makes solitude simpler. Downside is, it's a skeleton of the others, metal and plastic minus the stuffing and vinyl. Sure made my butt hurt but I got a panoramic view of everything we left behind. And after about three hundred loops I began to know exactly what was ahead by what had passed. Occasionally it changed—very occasionally. Like some days in the spring the sidewalks would be chalked with pink and blue hopscotch boards. And there were spider webs at Halloween and lights at Christmas and half-mast flags on dead days. Last year the Hendrixes moved into the old tudor on Branch Street. They painted the house dandelion yellow.

"The kids decided I had been the victim of a bad science experiment and could never go home. Not altogether untrue.

"She came to visit me twice.

"First time, she waited till all the kids were in school, got on the bus and promptly told me we were going to go sit by a pretty pond and make up, that apparently she was sorry and needed me back. I went. She asked me how I felt, what I thought, to for god sakes say something. I couldn't. She hugged me, then squeezed me tighter and tighter. I couldn't hug her back. She became angry at my lack of response and dunked my head under the water. She held my head there till the bubbles stopped surfacing and the little fight I mustered with my legs and neck had subsided. And then she pulled me out like a kitten by the scruff. She did mouth-to-mouth between sobbing and apologized over and over again.

"She led me by the spine back to the bus and left again. The next year went by very slowly. I couldn't bite my nails, smoke, rip out my hair, scratch my self or pick my nose. The no-arms thing was very impractical. Tia and I became very close during these years. She'd take me on most of her trips and we'd go exploring. She didn't mind that I couldn't talk and I didn't need arms for the journeys we went on.

"The second visit was different. She stood in front of the bus and held up both hands. The bus stopped. She got on, walked down row after row of ten-year-old children to the back and led me by the waist back down the same wide-eyed rows of children off the bus. We sat on the curb and she quietly held my shoulder and played with my hair. It felt nice. And then she looked sweetly into my eyes and quietly, gently asked where I lived. It was as if she'd seen me on a milk carton somewhere or read about me in a newspaper or editorial show, apparently no longer aware of being my sole custodian. I stared at her searchingly and not so sweetly pointed to the bus. We danced around each other a short time longer, her with words, me with bewildered, incredulous expressions she took to mean gratitude and stupidity. Shortly thereafter I reboarded the bus, alone.

"I am an eagle with chicken wings and a belly full of rocks.

"I am a unicorn prancing through the enchanted graveyard.

"I am a stripe-less skunk in the desert.

"I rode the bus for several months more before being whisked away by an older woman with bright red hair, a blue-checkered apron and a rolling pin. She kissed me on the top of my head and called herself Louisa. Humming brightly she took me into her kitchen, plunked me on the counter, opened the freezer and pulled out two frozen arms and a long windy thing I realized later were my vocal cords. She held my right arm up to my shoulder kissed their union and at once I could feel my fingertips cold and the blood rushing like a thousand motorcars to the latest attraction. She did the same with my left arm and then put my vocal cords into place with a tiny pair of salad tongs. And I sat there on the kitchen counter, my legs dangling shadows over the terra cotta tiles. I clapped and made a fist and punched the air and wiggled my fingers like worms. Louisa kissed me on the forehead and disappeared. I said thank you. And there it was, my voice.

"I screamed for joy. Nothing came out. I yelled in horror. Nothing. I tried pleading with God and please came out and thank you and what else can I do, how else can I be of assistance, what else do you need? And it was her. I was her. And I made a snowball, threw it at a tree and watched as midway down it lost momentum and then dimension and then my interest.

"So, back to the castle I went. I found her seated in her closet eating bon bons and I said in my most defiant voice that I was not a marionette and I needed control of my voice and arms back. She set down the chocolate and touched my arms and ran her forefinger over my lips. We stared at each other for a minute. "Louisa was by," I said and she just stared at me. "With the apron and rolling pin," I continued, staring at her until a thunderous voice from downstairs broke her gaze.

'When I say now, that means NOW! Said the Queen. 'There is a lot of work to be done!'

"She buried the chocolates in the back of the closet rather like a little squirrel and flew downstairs. I followed. She grabbed a broom, opened the front door and began sweeping the porch. Two kids walking down the street yelled, "Hey fatso." The queen walked up to her and stuck a pin right into the flesh above her heart. It read: Rise Above It. She started sweeping the front porch again.

'Pudgy wudgy woulda swam but she sank. Ta he he he he,' mocked the two marauders across the street.

And the queen came up and again stuck a pin into her chest. Blood squirted out. She watched. I winced. The queen smeared it away with the back of her hand. The new pin read: Turn The Other Cheek. She kept sweeping.

"I pushed past her, crossed the street and grabbed them each by the neck. "One more snot-nosed assholian remark and I'll shove your head right up your ass where it belongs." Nothing came out. I looked at her angrily and asked why she didn't say something to defend herself. She took a pin out of her pocket and stuck it on my forehead. It read: Be the Bigger Person.

"We lived with these three pins through sticks and stones and broken clones. We made it through three high schools, two colleges, a husband and about thirteen jobs. The pins ripped holes down to our belly buttons and eventually began breeding little pins that read: Perfect is Possible, Do More, Be the Best, Never Disappoint, Sacrifice Self and similar impossibilities.

"My only salvation was her weakness. She wouldn't acknowledge my existence but did allow me to very occasionally communicate our anger with the outside world. There were four conditions. She had to be under-nourished, sleep-deprived, over-stressed and outraged which usually was the result of some serious offense to basic human courtesy. Sample offenses: unthanked gobleshu's, unthanked doors held open—pretty much any form of thanklessness. Only at these times did she forget about the pins and let me speak for us both. I had to speak with my eyes and I perfected several looks: the Dagger, Twin Swords and Swarming Hornets. Important to build fear even if the intention has no viable consequence attached.

"It's all make-believe anyway is the conclusion I came to—a giant pretend sandbox filled with quicksand. I got in almost every day then, flailing my new-found arms and voice around in circus-like contortions waiting for someone to notice. This lasted for days that turned into years. And before long I forgot that the flailing went deeper than self-indulgent crazy making.

"I am the air in the wind of a deadly tornado.

"I am the blood in the frostbitten fingers of a purple hand.

"I am the budding leaf beneath the snow.

"Two years ago, I remembered I was angry. Prior to that she had me convinced we were crazy, or suffered from unpinpointable panic attacks or perhaps post traumatic stress syndrome or bipolar disorder or ocd or any of the other silly number of diagnosis she received. The big ugly "It" was her, her refusal to stand up for herself—to say no, I can't, I don't want to, I won't, I shouldn't have to, you suck, back off, get over it, let go, etc. I tried to tell her but she couldn't hear me. Damn vocal cords. I hated her. Hated her.

"And then quite out of nowhere Louisa reappeared. She baked batch after batch of faith cookies and I ate them like I'd never eaten anything before. They were better than chocolate or French fries or ice cream. After about three-hundred-and-eighty-five batches I began getting full. And that was the beginning, my true beginning.

"I am a full moon here, a new moon there.

"I am the blue clouds between the white sky.

"I have left the cocoon.

"Turns out Louisa's cookies had been feeding both of us. So, when I finally mustered the strength to speak with her again she was apologetic and eager to listen. She listened to everything I had to say. And I listened to her. And before long we were stating our mind. We felt anger and got angry. We felt injustice and demanded more. We felt lazy and did nothing. We tried to not be perfect, to not do more, to not be sensible. And for the first time in my life I felt heard. I felt important, purposeful. I had become the priority—over the queen and king, over the castle and all its subjects. We were an invincible team.

"And then a few months later ... whack! Smack! Sideswiped by economic disaster she fell down the cellar stairs and lay unconscious trapped again in the bowels of the castle. After years of being out, she was there again. Out of nowhere, there I was, back where I had begun. And it was different for a while but then it was the same. The queen had turned on herself and the king had turned up the pace of frenetic busy-making. The effect was silencing. She

couldn't hear me, couldn't respond. And when she came to, she was so trau-
matized by the fall she had forgotten how to say no. No became again synonymous with ungrateful bitch. And anger would mean the queen might freeze
her out and she'd have nowhere to go. And I began to panic ... flashbacks to
life before and then the homeless thing. And all I could think is gotta move
forward. Gotta get out. She's shutting down. Rooms are filling up with disappointment ... judgment ... fear. It's toxic and there are no doors. There's no
room to move, to even ... It's getting very stuffy ... can't breathe ... need air.
Can't find my windpipes to ... to ...

"Nights she was more peaceful. The castle quieted. So too did her mind. The
queen would take a short reprieve from self-sabotage and the King went to bed
early. One such night we were out stargazing—she, the queen and I. She
pointed to the stars and exclaimed how bright and beautiful and brilliant they
were. The queen watched and listened and nodded before flatly reminding her
that they didn't really exist. That the stars we can see are actually dead. They
are nothing but a sparkling illusion far, far removed from a non-existent reality. It is important not to be fooled, to know what is real and what is not and
not to waste your energy reaching for things that don't exist. And she looked
at the queen paralyzed by the logic, the sense, the deadening truth. And then I
reminded her that it wasn't ours. Her truth wasn't ours.

"And somehow she got it. Our truth was different. And our truth made her re-
forgot the reality she had remembered and re-remember the reality she'd forgotten. The royals were governed by a history of unrelenting seasons. And an
early spring was not expected. So we decided to move our June. And finally it
was ours to move," she said quietly yawning at the journey she had just
relayed.

I felt completely exhausted too, like a giant train or I guess more appropriately
yellow school bus had hit me. I had been so cruel, so torturously, suffocatingly
unforgiving and deaf. It was a miracle that Wanda, that all my inner voices
were still willing to speak to me. I hadn't realized till now, till right now how

really incredibly lucky I was to be listening, to be having this undeserved but beautiful opportunity to listen.

And it clicked more boldly than anything had.
Mothering was about listening—not always just to what is said
but to the deeper meanings behind it,
the truth inside it

Shadow of My Words

She listened not to what I said
but the shadow of my words
and in their shifting shapes
things that can't be heard,
and in their shifting shapes
things that can't be heard.

And there beneath the I'm not angry
and rage—well that's absurd
beneath the smile, behind the eyes
the list of well-intentioned lies,
beyond the things I said
she heard the voices in my head.

She saw beyond my platitudes
to swallowed bits of blue
It didn't happen in a day
took a while to finally say.
But somewhere in my tired sighs
she saw the sign of quiet smiles.

Yeah, she listened not to what I said
but the shadow of my words
and in their shifting shapes
things that can't be heard,

and in their shifting shapes
things that can't be heard.

And off to the side of no big deal
and anything you want
left of kindness, down from joy
somewhere left of coy
she heard the voices in my head
beyond the things I said.

And there in 14J
I somehow lost my way
and found amidst the scattered debris
a ray of possibility
a hope that I could someday be
finally free of me.

Yeah, she listened not to what I said
but the shadow of my words
and in their shifting shapes
things that can't be heard,
and in their shifting shapes
things that can't be heard.

I am winter seeds awaiting spring …

I crave the patience to be willing to wait, to have faith that my spring will come and my album will blossom and to know this deep down in my bones, the way winter's branches know that green will again run through their veins and flowers be born from their fingers. Despite the ice-encrusted months buried in snow and freezing weather, looking like scraggly dried-up garbage there is this ultimate, instinctual knowing nature has that allows it to rest and recover and replenish its' strength and to be able to do this because it knows, knows where the coming months will take it.

And I am missing this kind of inner faith. I can do the self pep talk, no problem—give it to myself or any one who needs it. But there is not the knowing in my heart, in that place deep down that everything will work out, that it will all be okay. And I don't mean in some silly pansy, bed of roses, bowl of cherries kind of way. There is a look in some peoples' eyes, people who truly know their life's destiny, know all the way down in their soul that whatever happens there is this thing they will do, this gift they will give the world or their family or something—there is this "knowing" that you can tell guides them, guides their decisions. Their actions are not created. Their plans are not contrived. It all comes from within. And then out.

I crave this kind of knowing. Because what I have come to know is that with all the most brilliant planning in the world things never work out quite according to plan. And though there's always something to gain, there is a slow-building distrust that wells up as to what can really be accomplished by doing the very most and being the very best you can. It is not that I believe in fate or like ultimately we have no control. But, it does seem sometimes like free will is something different than I had imagined, that it is tied to a different set of principles than hard work and perseverance, that in the end free will comes down to a set of criteria that seems to be higher order.

And this brings me back to the whole knowing thing. I always of think of knowing as based on knowledge and I am coming to realize I am absolutely right and completely wrong. It is knowledge but not the way I have always thought—not quantifiable, provable, logical knowledge but more the knowledge of trust, faith—like an inner GPS tracking device that only comes from tuning in to frequencies no one else can really teach you because no one else is going to your particular destination. And certainly no one else, at least yet, can quantify or prove. And this kind of knowledge, despite my nearly prayerful listening, I don't seem to have. My faith is limited to what I can do, not what I have it in me to be. And I fear without this part I will never be what I want to be, accomplish what I dream of accomplishing.

But I cannot give up because there is this driving force, perhaps the cousin of faith that will not let me let go. And so as I try to hang on and understand or more appropriately intuit. I will listen again and I suppose again and again and again. But this time I will try not to listen for what I want to hear or think I need to hear. I will listen for what I know somewhere deep inside.

Supergirl

"Swish!!! Swooosh!!!!! And Kablooey Kabang!!!!! I am the one, the only, the liveliest little sprite of a superhero you'll ever know, Supergirl. I have no cape as you can see, but I do have this forty-foot checkered scarf and a watch with my name, Supergirl, engraved right in it. Well, you can't see the engraving because it is done in Supergirl script to protect me but it's there. And I have my own cartoon strip that runs after me, documenting my every move. I am immensely famous and I've been asked to give you a tour. Come on …

"Thwack!!!!! Wangaluckachangit!!!!! I run up against all kinds of resistance. For instance right now there's an army of bunny monkey clones trying to capture me and make me their evil princess slave. They've launched a radioactive isotope attack Yeeeeeeeeeeeeeks!!!!!! from their underground Neptune bunkers. Defending against them takes a good part of my day after which I can attempt to rescue the rest of the world from the endless evils threatening it," she said barely pausing to inhale.

I wasn't at all sure she was going to get the knowing thing. Seemed just the slightest bit frivolous. But, I'd hang in there. Had paid off so far. Eventually it was bound to sink in.

"What do I do during the rest of the day?" she asked. "Well, there are all kinds of toxic energy rings that need battling. Kepowpowppowpow!!!! Leftover, unresolved anger auras that need radical reconstructive obliterating. It's like emotional sandblasting. First I have to scan every micro-millimeter of their invisible walls. This requires my X-ray goggles. And even then I have to feel around to see where they've inserted the deadly titanium stopper into the Power Source—Ick!!!! And Ughhh!!!!—and remove it before it stunts the growth of our earthly evolution.

"After that the ring begins its molecular breakdown followed right after by a subatomic disintegration into anger dust which when banded together with my intergalactic glue gun makes super-powered fertilizer which I use exclusively to feed graveyard love. Imagine—all from toxic energy rings. Wamba Momba!!!!!

"They're just like Saturn's rings except you can't see them even by telescope. And although the crusty exterior is always made of toxic anger, the insides vary quite a lot. There is the goopy sticky stuff of deep melancholia, the neon oozy gel of envy, the foul-smelling stink of backed-up martyrdom, the spurting fumes of guilt and the tangled rat's nest of resentment. Well, that's the top five. The list is too long to list.

"Ring rousting takes most of my morning so sometimes I have to come back in the late afternoon—Grrrr.... ughhhhhh!!!!! to round up the fertilizer. Depends on the size of the ring. Then I usually go for lunch, which consists of a half carafe of lava. "Mmmmmmmmmm ... I call it passion juice and it sure does get the juices flowing. Solids slow me down so I stick to an all-liquid diet. Lava lunch is crucial because I spend the afternoon melting karmic paralysis. And let me tell you it is backbreaking work. There are thousands of past lives in each current soul that need five-star red alarm help. The downtown area alone could take me a lifetime (of which, by the way, I have many) but I need to hunker down and focus only on the ones that have venomous paralyzing power.

"I look for giant icebergs in the psychic field and then spit on them with my lava-laced saliva. Spitattletooeytuck!!!!!!!!! They break down differently but always melt away in relief revealing an ice sculpture of the original problem. I take snapshots with my heart shutter and send them via c-mail (that's "c" as in cosmic) to their angels or guides or whosever shift it is. Used to try and relay the problem directly but art is always subject to interpretation and the guides are degreed in that area. So, I stick with picture taking.

"I have no boss. Well, no big mean outside boss. Well, not outside. Actually, I do. But, I'd call them more co-collaborators or compatriots for the cause. If you want to get very technical about it I do report to them on a bi-annual, tri-weekly and every other daily basis. When you get really good and they believe in you one hundred percent, they check in on you hourly. That, I can't imagine. Whooooo ... wheeeeeee!!!!!!!!!! There are several offices. There's one in Medulla, one in Aorta and one in Gutsylvania.

"I used to favor the Medulla office in my early years as Supergirl. Always knew what to expect. But after being sent down to Aorta for my every other day meetings I found my relief sculptures improving, my lava heat tolerance increasing and my general mood to be a bit less grumpy. I check in voluntarily with the Gutsylvania office, which is all the way downtown near the bowel of it all. They are abrupt and perfunctory and usually filled with exactly the news you were hoping not to hear. Ughhhhhhhhhhhh!!!!!!!!!!!!!! But after the first million or so visits it becomes comforting. And there's not the elusive, unactionable advice you get from Aorta or the circular sprally advice of Medulla. What you see is what you get is the real deal—make no bones about it. At my Supergirl inauguration I was told if I work very hard for these three offices, eventually they would end up working for me. Yippeeeeeeeeeeeeeeeeeeeeeeeeeee!!!!!!!!!!!!!!!!!!

"So, it is my current Supergirl Plan to do a little less each day and check in a little more. But for now back to fertilizing the graveyard."

I am winter seeds awaiting spring ...

She knew she didn't know
but had faith that something inside her did.
And that somehow, no matter what happened
when or how or why, she'd be alright.
She was given signs along the way,
signs she saw.

Send Me Fireflies

Nothing's as it seems
running sideways down this dream.
Been feeling lately like it might work out.
Smiling through the haze
of these disconnected days
Not sure of what tomorrow's about.
Knowing and not the line ...
how it shifts in time.
Can't seem to find my way out
night-time fills with doubt.

Send me fireflies at midnight
something that says it will be alright,
modest beacon of light,
Send me fireflies at midnight
something that says it'll be alright,
that's it still worth the fight.

Where'm'I supposed to go ...
how'm I supposed to know
all the little thing I don't?
Something has to give

All the Girls

live and letting live
getting what you really want.
Can't pay before you leave
in foreign currency.
You only make believe
You know what sets you free.

Send me fireflies at midnight
something that says it will be alright,
modest beacon of light,
Send me fireflies at midnight
something that says it'll be alright,
that it's still worth the fight.

Can't seem to find my way out
nighttime fills with doubt
peeling back the layers of truth
for unmistakable proof
forgetting what you know
learning to let go …

Send me fireflies at midnight
something that says it will be alright,
modest beacon of light,
Send me fireflies at midnight
something that says it'll be alright,
that it's still worth the fight.

I am a Kiss Blown into the Wind ...

And, so, I guess in the end, like in all ends, it begins again. There will always be more questions, more problems, more opportunities, more searching—and more voices.

Such a wildly rewarding pilgrimage to have embarked on—this listening. Feels like years have gone by. And I suppose in some sense they have, a lifetime of years. And I feel older and yet younger and quietly full of infinite energy and passionately full of patience. It is a strange and upside down feeling but good and truthful. And the truthful feeling is strange too. I thought I'd felt it many times before—like an amazing epiphany. But this time it feels small and humble and infinitely more valuable.

And having taken such a strange and intimate trip together it feels odd not to lean in and ask how it was for you, if it wore you down or lifted you up, if you heard any of your own voices and if it is not too personal, what did they say? But our relationship being what it is may I just say thank you for listening and express my deepest hope that you listen out for the rich and beautiful voices that make up your extraordinary personal symphony.

So, to close the loop on where we started out, the good news is the dogs have not been kicked to death by the donkeys. Cornelia is dating someone and become a bit less chatty. Our nanny was not deported. We've hired a new contractor who as of yet hasn't embezzled any money and seems confident we will get back on track for around our budget. (Yes, I know what this really means but better to start here, right?) And most important, sleep, although still very much a luxury, is mine a few nights a week.

On a more challenging note … our lease has run out and the house isn't done so we are off to another rental, our nanny quit to go into the restaurant business. I have to decide about whether to go back to work and what to do regarding my album. And oh yes, on the amazingly joyful side, I am pregnant again.

So there continue to be joys and struggles and challenges. Hardship, sadness, things I am sure I could never imagine will come my way. But as long as there continue to be these voices, as long as I stay in touch with all the girls, there will always be answers. And not redundant perfunctory answers but deeply inspiring and original answers. And they will fill my lyrics with life and make my life more lyrical.

I settled on this thought for a while and before too long it made its way into a feeling that swelled inside my chest like the late summer sun, all wistful and warm and sweetly uncertain. We are not reducible to a single voice. We are complex and fluid and broken … into the most beautiful mosaics.

978-0-595-44284-3
0-595-44284-6

LaVergne, TN USA
02 November 2009
162766LV00005B/27/A